LETTERS TO JANE

LETTERS TO JANE

Hayden Carruth

AUSABLE PRESS
2004

Cover art: "Turkey-Tail Fungi" (photograph)
by Dr. Darlyne A. Murawski
National Geographic Image Collection/Getty Images

Design and composition by Ausable Press
The type is Perpetua with Perpteua LT Titling.
Cover design by Rebecca Soderholm

Published by
AUSABLE PRESS
1026 HURRICANE ROAD
KEENE, NY 12942
www.ausablepress.org

Distributed to the trade by:
CONSORTIUM BOOK SALES & DISTRIBUTION
1045 WESTGATE DRIVE
SAINT PAUL, MN 55114-1065
(651) 221-9035
(651) 221-0124 (FAX)
(800) 283-3572 (ORDERS)

The acknowledgments appear on page 111 and constititute a
continuation of the copyright page.

Library of Congress Cataloging-in-Publication Data
Carruth, Hayden, 1921—
Letters to Jane / Hayden Carruth. —1st ed.
p. cm.
Hayden Carruth's letters to Jane Kenyon between April 1994 and April 1995,
the year she was dying.
ISBN 1-931337-17-9 (hardcover: alk. paper)
ISBN 1-931337-18-7 (pbk. : alk. paper)
1. Terminally ill–United States–Biography. 2. Terminal care–Patients–Biography.
I. Kenyon, Jane. II. Title
R726.8.C396 2004
616'.029'092–dc22
2004010640

April 25, 1994

Dear Jane,

It's an entirely typical morning here. Gray, drizzly, warm, a song sparrow in the old grape vine, crows congregating noisily in the woods. I've been up for about an hour and a half. I've made coffee and fed the cats, Mudgins and Cooker, I've drunk two mugs of coffee and smoked six or seven cigarettes, I've considered my sins, and now I'm sitting in my tattered old wingback chair by the stove (cold at this time of year) with my new portable computer on my knees. Much more comfortable than sitting stark upright at the desk. Joe-Anne is still sleeping. We were up late last night, as we are most nights.

We heard the rumor of your illness a couple of weeks ago, but from a source I thought might not be reliable. We were thinking of ways to confirm or disconfirm it without asking directly, which seemed too clumsy, and finally Joe-Anne wrote Don a letter that he would have to answer—he would have anyway, of course—and now we know. We've both been devastated. We've wept and raged. Of all the blows to our sense of propriety and natural rectitude that we've sustained in the past few years, this is the worst by far. I don't know what to say. I know you are in pain and extremely uncomfortable, so I can't wish you anything on that account. I know you are courageous and stubborn. I know you are remarkably intelligent and that your intelligence is the kind which includes good sense. I know your mind possesses immense resources of imaginative energy. About all I can do (unless you tell me otherwise) is reassure you of our love, Joe-Anne's and mine. It is compounded of natural affinity, gratitude, and admiration. It is great and active.

I remember the first time you and I met, at least I think it was the first, before I met you with Don. You were doing a reading in Syracuse. We had lunch together at a restaurant called O'Toole's, where the dining area is a balcony surrounding a lower room in which the bar is located. It bothered my acrophobia, and we sat at a table as far from the railing as we could get. Immediately we knew we were kin, so to speak. We talked about psychogenic disabilities in a tough, laughing way, comparing experiences. It was a reinforcing thing for us, warm with the bonding that comes from mutuality of suffering and temperament—I think I had already reviewed a couple of your books—the sort of understanding that revives instantaneously whenever and however infrequently we meet, as it has.

Don't think about answering this. Use your good time for getting strong and writing poems. I will write again soon. Tomorrow I must go down to D.C. to do a reading, about which I'm a little apprehensive because I was in the hospital myself recently for an operation and don't feel altogether up to it, but I'm sure I'll be all right and I'll be back home the next day.

With love,

[signature]

April 29, 1994

Dear Jane,

I'm in the waiting area at the Washington National Airport with another hour before boarding for my flight to Syracuse. I hate this place, I hate it. Hatred has not been a prominent factor in my life, but in this particular place at this particular time it is. The weather here is INTOLERABLE, hot, hot, hot, and coming from Upstate New York I'm not dressed for it, wearing my faithful tweed jacket that I customarily use for readings. And I've had three glasses of house chardonnay in one of those little cubicles off the waiting area, the only place where one is permitted to smoke. I woke up this morning in the hotel and could not figure out where I was. What is this place!? How could I be here? Christ! Where is Joe-Anne, where is the Bo? Then of course I came to full consciousness and wished like hell I were back asleep.

Well, I'll insert a "poem" I wrote while I was having my coffee and so-called croissant:

IN GEORGETOWN

Holiday Inn, Washington, D.C.
This is not where the rich and famous pursue their
    lifestyles.
This is exactly like the Holiday Inn in Troy, N.Y. where I
    stayed recently.
It is near enough to exactly like the Holiday Inn where I
    stayed in Tucson,
In Casper, in Chillecothe, in Opelika, in Portsmouth, in
    Bellingham, etc.
A mirror in a fake gilt frame, brass bed-lamps attached to
    the wall by hinges.
"Fax Your Urgent Documents To or From This Holiday
    Inn Hotel."
From time to time the smoke alarm goes off for no
    reason. Eeeeeeeeeeee!

Thumps on the door, an anxious black lady. "Are you all
    right in there, sir?"
I climb up on a brocaded chair and disconnect the smoke
    alarm ruthlessly.
Meanwhile the rich and famous are pursuing their
    lifestyles two blocks away
In their cute four-story federal brick houses with
    porticoes and flagstone steps.
Fucking each other's wives in the dens and laundry rooms
    and pantries.
This is called a party. Some are Democrats, some Repub-
    licans, all are fuckers.
They are emboldened by bourbon and vodka and the
    anticipation of power.
Tomorrow they will arise hungover and wield the
    resources of the nation.
Sweetheart, it's a long way from home, miles and miles
    from your warm bed.
Melodiously at the door: "Are you all right, sir? Are you
    all right in there?"

No literature, whatever that is. A mess of words analogous to
a mess of feeling.

Well, my dear, why am I complaining to you? Is com-
plaint the endless, relentless motif of our time? Can I imagine
a poem or a symphony entirely devoted to joyousness and
exaltation, like those of the 19th century? No, I cannot. Tak-
ing into account my own innate pessimism, I still cannot
imagine it.

I am at your bedside. I am holding your hand. I am looking

into your beautiful eyes. I have an impulse to stroke your head, your lovely curly half-gray hair, but am uncertain if it would be acceptable. Jane, I am so overcome by the power and sweetness of your poems, the power and sweetness of your complicated self, that I am reduced to mental and emotional paralysis. With one foot in the grave myself, there is nothing else. We are falling through the hourglass, grains of sand drifting down. I hope and believe that you will beat this affliction—many people have—but I know that in my condition I will scarcely have a chance to see you again. But I see you. I hear you. I even touch you. (Don will not mind.) I have great affection for you in my mind and heart. (Joe-Anne won't mind either.) I embrace you, I tottering with my gnarled walking stick. We have done so much, we have each in our way put down on paper or on the filaments of the common mind words of goodness, of human love in the midst of so much human evil and murderousness—we are in some sense special. In history's best sense, if there is such a thing. I believe in your perceptive tenacity. I hold your hand for what strength I can give in the struggle. Very little. Yet I have confidence. You are going to beat this illness, this mark of metaphysical adversity, as many, many powerful women have beat it before you.

I will print this out and mail it to you when I get home.

Love to Don. With love,

𝒳?

April 30, 1994

Dear Jane,

I arrived in Syracuse at about 5:00 yesterday but somehow was waylaid by friends who plied me with pineapple juice and hors d'oeuvres made from dogfood and bits of coal until I was utterly stinko. I am still in Syracuse. Joe-Anne will come and get me later on. I am sitting in a leather easy chair with my feet on a fine Bokara carpet, smoking cigarettes, drinking coffee and whiskey, my little computer, which is called "Hayden's Toy," plugged into the wall beside me—one's constant connection. Where would we be without our baseboard outlets? The house is empty except for me and one delightful child named Clio, who is upstairs in bed with a fever. No one seems to know what's the matter with her. General dissatisfaction, I expect.

I think of us, our little gang, as refugees, not so much from the world, which used to be our enemy but now just ignores us, as from the "literary community," which fears us. I saw this in Washington. Very nice young people who treated me well, but I could tell from their questions that what they really want is for me to get out of the way, me with my old-fashioned notions of honesty and compassion. "How can you possibly love a heron?" they say. "Such a ridiculous, filthy bird—and obsolete at that." And how can I answer? My poems convince them momentarily; their eyes shine, their faces blush. But then in an instant they recover themselves and reject all my nonsense.

Incidentally I have become a splendid performer. Who could have foreseen that? It surprises everyone who knows me, including myself. I didn't give my first reading until I was 58 years old.

Well, the lady of the house, Isabel, who is a Chilean refugee and whom I love dearly, has come home for lunch and Joe-Anne will be here before long. Members of the little gang. I could not survive without them.

Love again,

𝓔,

May 9, 1994

Dear Jane,

Monday morning. Warm and bright. At this time of day the sun shines through the kitchen window and hits my chair. So I bask like a cat while I'm having my coffee and cigarettes. Joe-Anne is down in Jersey to see her family, especially her son Adam, and I'm alone for a couple of weeks, which always makes me haywire—depressed and desperate at the same time. I know you know what I mean. (Joe-Anne doesn't want me to go with her on these visits and I've never met any of her family except Adam—but that's another story.) So I frittered away the weekend: read a short manuscript, wrote a few letters, watched a hell of a lot of basketball, read what we used to call cheap-screw fiction. I haven't heard that term for a while. At first it meant under-the-counter porn, but later came to mean any escapist literature. As a consequence, on top of the desperation and depression I feel guilt. What else is new?

Well, it's the start of a new week and maybe I can get myself on track.

It's tulip time and I've seen some marvelous displays in people's yards, including a couple in my own. It's also insect time. The black flies up in the woods are fierce, the house has been invaded by new legions of ants and spiders. When I woke this morning a small, very delicate spider was on the wall about six inches from my head. I put on my glasses and looked at it. Long graceful legs like a ballet dancer's. Unafraid and poised. I blew at it gently and I swear it turned around and looked at me, though even with my glasses I couldn't see its eyes. A nice little greeting in the morning from the world to me. I'm reminded of when I was a soldier in Italy 50 years or more ago. We used to sleep in mosquito bars because of the malaria (which most of us got anyway), and often in the morning when I woke up there'd be a little Italian lizard on the netting about six inches above my face. Looking, at that distance, like a dinosaur. Another nice little greeting. If you moved very slowly you could sometimes tickle their bellies and they seemed to like it.

Well, the cats are demanding their breakfast. Their proper names are Cookie (because she is black and white like an Oreo, named by Adam when she was a kitten) and Smudge (because she is all white except for a little gray patch on her head that wouldn't wash off when I took her in as a filthy starved waif three years ago), but normally they are called Cooker and Mudgins. Cooker is a very old cat now and has metal replacements in her hind quarters from the time when she was hit by a car, so she walks with a wobble and complains from time to time; but she's still good-looking and very affectionate. Mudgins is handsome, in the prime of life, haughty, superior, yet she follows me around like a dog and always stays within sight distance. When I'm working she sleeps on my worktable. I'm thinking about getting a dog, which I've wanted ever since

I came to Munnsville. I've held off because the highway that runs past our house is heavily traveled by cars and trucks going at high speed and I've seen too many animals killed on the wayside. But perhaps I can find a way to overcome that risk. It will take patience. But I have this summer mostly free to stay at home, and training a dog would be a good thing to do.

Jane, I know you're going through every kind of hell. I know there's nothing I can say about it that you don't know. I'm as sorry as I can be, devastated, and I'm thinking of you a lot. I hope my silly letters don't seem offensive to you.

With much love,

May 13, 1994

Dear Jane,

In spite of the good news from South Africa and one or two other hopeful developments, something ominous is going on—or am I simply a pessimist and skeptic? The radio is going in the other room, tuned to the morning news program on the public station. Stories about invasions of Haiti are surfacing, it seems, followed by blanket denials from the government. Will Bill Clinton turn out to be just as devious and savage as Nixon or Reagan or Johnson? A moment ago I had a flash of vision in which I saw Clinton's face twisted by the same rictus of greed, shame, and brutality we've seen on other presidents in our time. It struck me that within a few days or weeks we are in for another sudden announcement of the kind we have come to know all too well.

Not that I have any solution to the ghastly problems in Haiti, except that I deplore the policy of sending back the escapees.

Last night I gave a reading at the Oneida Community Mansion House, which along with the Oneida Community silver business is what remains of one of the most radical utopian experiments of the last century. It's about ten miles over the hill from Munnsville. The community was founded by a fellow named Noyes, first name I think Josiah, who like Joseph Smith came from Vermont—I can't remember which town. He believed in total 100% communism. All the members of the community lived and worked together without distinctions of gender, marriage, ability, age, etc., and all the property was owned in common. One result is that the local phone book has more people named Noyes than any others, because so many children were born in the community with no way to tell who their fathers were: so they were named after the founder. A friend and neighbor of mine here in Munnsville is Paul Noyes, who has no idea who his grandfather was. The reading was all right, even though I'd felt especially lousy all day. I had a snort or two of Jack Daniels beforehand. The audience was about one third composed of elderly women who live in the Mansion (and probably have no idea who their grandfathers were either, nor perhaps even their grandmothers) and obviously they were there because they have nothing else in the world to do. Nevertheless they seemed to enjoy the reading and I did a pretty fair job of it. The building is an enormous house with 200 rooms designed in the Italianate style, not Palladian but more like a huge villa with brick and tile and strange twisting corridors, little tight stairways, fancy doors, a very nice little auditorium that holds about 100 people, a kitchen which produces the best food in Oneida County. Strange. The community broke up in about 1900 because the silversmithing business was so successful that disputes arose, even before the death of Noyes, about who would manage the finances. The business, long since incorporated (i.e., owned by private individuals), still flourishes and has factories all over the world. It keeps the Mansion going, along with grants from local arts and humanities foundations.

It was a strange place to live, the scene of so much hope, so much failure. On the walls were group photographs from a century ago, including large numbers of children dressed like Tom Sawyer and Becky Thatcher. Their anxious faces. Were they wondering who their fathers were? Or didn't they care? A crucial question in political philosophy, but I don't know that anyone knows the answer, or even if there is an answer.

I still feel lousy. What the hell's the point of giving a poetry reading to 75 people in a superannuated house in Oneida, N.Y.? I think I'll go into Syracuse and spend the weekend with Isabel and Stephen if I can get the Bo to look after things here.

It's a crisp day here, windy, lots of fast-moving cumulus, after frost last night. When I got home from the reading I had to bring in my impatiens and geraniums. Today the tulips, big and hearty and colorful, are tight-petaled, looking huddled and bulbous. Many are bowed down from the wind and rain. It's about 40° outside and I have the furnace running. I wish I had fuel for the woodstove, but I've run out.

Much love, always,

May 19, 1994

Dear Jane,

I am sitting here contemplating the mess on the kitchen floor that has resulted from my bringing in two hanging plants, a red and a pink impatiens, last week against the frost and then going off to Syracuse to recover from a predictable case of the jimmerish jimmies. The cats love flowers, particularly Mudgins. She loves to eat them. So leaves and buds are scattered all around. The plants have survived, I think, and I've put them back outdoors. I seem to have survived too, and am feeling abashed and contrite, as usual, and I'll clean up the mess this afternoon before Joe-Anne gets home.

Then we may have a greater mess because she is bringing a dog with her. One of two that her family wants to farm out for a while, maybe forever. But I don't know which of the two will come. "Let it be a surprise," Joe-Anne said. Well, I've wanted a dog for a long time, so in a way I'm looking forward to this, though in another I'm not because the cats have had this house to themselves for several years and I'm apprehensive about what will happen when a big, barky intruder appears on the scene. Further bulletins about that will be forthcoming.

My daughter Martha had another liver operation yesterday. In Birmingham. She is ok, but woozy.

I just saw an indigo bunting at my feeder, along with two cardinals and three goldfinches. Very colorful. A happy change from the wretched cowbirds that usually monopolize the place.

Thanks for the card. I hadn't known about Don's dog/cat book, which seems altogether apropos—the book, I mean—at this moment in this house. I'll get a copy.

Meanwhile the weather here, as no doubt in Wilmot, has been dark and damp for quite a while. My pear and cherry trees are in bloom, but the apples are struggling. The grass is growing like fury. Such an immense change from a month ago, it's always astonishing. I look out across the valley and see the big arras of rich greens where white sterility prevailed for so long, with deep brown plowed fields here and there, and I am unexpectedly moved. This is my 73rd springtime. Isn't it great that one has this capacity for renewed response in spite of everything.

I'll enclose two snapshots that Jean V. sent me. Probably you've already seen them, or similar ones. She is trying to entice me to visit Ireland, which I'd be glad to do if I could afford it and if I had a slave to take care of all the arrangements and deliver me to the airplane at the right time and place. I do like the look of the country in these pictures; no doubt because it reminds me of Vermont, the stony pastures on the farms I knew there. But of course we had no ocean to lend piquancy to the air. I never missed it, to say the truth, but perhaps if we'd had it I would have enjoyed it.

Now I must get on with the day's chores. More soon.

Much love, always,

彦,

May 20, 1994

Dear Jane,

Joe-Anne returned last night, and with her came Stacey— that's what I've decided to call her. It's not the name she has borne heretofore, which I don't like, but close enough; she

15

recognizes it. She resembles a somewhat overgrown red fox. I'd say she must have some Irish setter in her background, but she's a good deal smaller than a setter and must have a lot of other things in her too. Her ears stand up but not pointedly, her eyes are brown, so is her nose, she has a fine brushy tail, etc. The main thing is that she is very friendly, took to me and this house immediately, spent the night placidly, seems unperturbed by her sudden transplantation.

The cats are another matter. Cooker has stayed in the kitchen and doesn't mind Stacey as long as she doesn't come too near, and then she, Cooker, hisses and lashes out. Mudgins has remained upstairs the whole time so far, ready to dash under the bed if danger approaches. I don't like this; dissension in the house of any kind always upsets me. I'm hoping that peace will be restored soon and I'm doing what I can—not much—to promote it.

It's a beautiful day here, after a week of dark rainy weather. The pansies I planted in a box on the stoop look awful. Maybe today will give them strength if not hope, which inhabitants of Upstate New York know better than to entertain. I will move a couple of big flourishing geraniums outdoors today but will wait to move my hibiscus, which is seven feet high and has six blossoms on it. It looms over my table in the workroom, giving me the illusion of working in the woods all winter.

Much love, as ever,

May 26, 1994

Dear Jane,

Another dark damp morning. (The time noted above is that of printing, not writing.) The rain has knocked down the apple-blossoms, which is too bad, they were glorious while they lasted, great puffs of light surrounding the house. And we did have three or four days of fair weather in which to enjoy them. The tulips have also fallen, except for a few late ones here and there. The lilacs are full and beautiful. One of our lilac trees, the biggest, has the dark purple blossoms I like best, which are brilliant when the light is effulgent, a great burgeoning beyond the kitchen window.

I've been reading manuscripts for a poetry prize, not as many this time as in the past—I guess the screening process is more stringent than it used to be. But I haven't found a single book I can be enthusiastic about. I wish now I hadn't agreed to do it, because it puts me in a bind: I've already received and cashed the check, and I must choose a winner, I must write a statement about it, I must have my name attached to it. Which means, in effect, I must tell a lie and be a hypocrite. Of course I could write a check and turn down the assignment, late as it is. But that would bother me a lot too, it's not my style. Damn. These manuscripts—anonymous, but equally divided between women and men—are frightfully stylish and clever and Cantabridgian. Anyway to me they are, for all their brilliance, dry as dust, trivial, pretentious, over-refined, and unrewarding. Not the direction in which our poetry should be moving at this point—or at any point. Well, today I must make a choice, write the obligatory paragraph about it, and send off the whole thing to the authorities, and I swear I shall never do anything like this again. I've sworn this before a good many times, of course. Then someone calls me on the phone and I don't have enough backbone to say no. My fault. But not really. Although occasionally the telephone is a great boon, no doubt of that, all in all I wish it had never been invented.

During the good weather I planted pansies, sweet william, petunias, moved the big geraniums outdoors, hung a couple of pots of impatiens from the porch roof. And we've had an indigo bunting at our feeder each evening for a week, around 6:30 faithfully. The first time I've seen one come so close. We have plenty of color around us, in other words, and it's grateful to the eye, as my father used to say.

Much love,

𝒢,

May 31, 1994

Dear Jane,

The last day of May, and without doubt the first day of summer. It's hot! At least it feels hot to me, quite hellish, though three-quarters of the people in the world would say it's merely comfortable and mild. Even when I was a kid I disliked the summer; now I dread it. Something to do with metabolism? Yesterday my son the Bo set up my air-conditioner in the bedroom upstairs, so if it gets too fierce I can retire up there, taking my portable computer with me. What luxury.

Anyway the spring is gone, or nearly. The apple and pear blossoms have fallen, tulips likewise. The lilac is our chief source of color now, and it is beautiful. It's a medium-sized tree (bush), probably 20 or 30 years old, but the kind that has the deep purple, not bluish, blossoms, and though I generally don't take to hybrids, I do like this, it's so rich and strong. This year the blossoms are especially abundant. Otherwise we have the spirea hedge that runs along the front of our place—except that really we have no front, the only door to this house is the kitchen door. The hedge hasn't been trimmed for over a year and the heavy snow last winter broke and bent many of the stems. It looked ratty and ragged before the blossoms came. Now it looks splendid. Creamy white in the moonlight when I went to bed at 3:00 AM.

Ain't nature grand!

Last week on Friday and Saturday we visited Francine Prose and her husband Howie Michels at their place in Krumville, NY, which is near Woodstock on the other side of the Catskills from here. I don't know if you know Francine and her work. Myself, I only know Francine. I've never read any of her books. And I'm pretty sure she has never read any of mine. It's strange in a way, but delightful too: two writers who haven't read each other's work and are content— more than content—to be friends on a simply human level. I like her immensely. And I like Howie too, he's a painter and sculptor and has a big old barn that he uses for a gallery and studio, full of wonderful things. I guess his work is not popular because it is roughly figurative and expressionist, but I find some of it quite moving. They have an old 18th century farmhouse that has been restored with a very big, glass-enclosed room added on, a delightful room full of light and greenery, including the biggest philodendron I've seen in years—it's on a pallet on castors so they can roll it around and turn it easily. That's typical of them. Howie is a fine carpenter and cabinet-maker as well as a painter and he has made most of their furniture and many handy little gadgets around the house. The drive to and from Krumville across the heart of the Catskills was very pleasant too. I had my eye out for lilacs. Saw a great many of them, of course. But none I liked better than my own, which is always gratifying. Also saw a huge number of lawn sales, garage sales, etc., I estimated at least 150 between Krumville and Munnsville, and that was gratifying too: at least I'm not out there on the roadside trying to peddle my junk to someone else who doesn't need it.

Krumville/Munnsville. A couple of plain-sounding towns if there ever were any. It must be nice to live in Wilmot. I seem to land easily in plain-sounding towns. The only thing I didn't much like about my 20 years in Vermont was the name of the town where I lived, Johnson. Surrounded by Craftsbury, Stowe, St. Albans and other fine-sounding places. During the administration of Lyndon Johnson I used to date my letters from Jimson.

Yesterday in the woods with Stacey I found a May apple in perfect flower, the shy white beautiful blossom hidden under the big leaves. It reminded me of you.

With love,

June 7, 1994

Dear Jane,

For the past couple of years we've had what we call a "horned finch" at our feeder, viz. a female house finch with a tuft of feathers on either side of her head, just above her eyes. Now we have four of them! We wonder if we are starting a new subspecies, Darwin in action. Or perhaps this isn't the anomaly it seems and we are simply ignorant; our bird books don't help. Anyway we are constantly (almost) entertained by this. It's one of those little natural enigmas that keep daily life going and fuel our stamina, a focus, a triangle: husband, wife, bird—a source, a resource. Of what? God knows. One of us will look out the window and say, "There she is," whereupon the other will look out and say, "Yes, there she is"—and what could be sillier? Is it because we are a childless couple and have nothing on which to concentrate our mutual energy? I wouldn't be surprised. And when I consider the children of my younger friends, especially the adolescent children, I'm not at all unhappy about it.

I'll be going down to Pennsylvania tomorrow to give a reading and seminar at Lehigh on Thursday and already I'm feeling nervous, as usual. That edge of uncertainty which I'm sure you share with me before such things. I'll be fine, of course. I almost always am. I take a gulp of whiskey and a Propranolol half an hour ahead of time and get up there with amazing aplomb, then I read a funny poem that makes everyone laugh, the same poem nearly every time, and from there on it's a breeze. But the truth is that even though I've been doing public readings for only a few years I've become a performer now, not a poet, and I think about this somewhat regretfully. I do the dialect poems very well, and I do the lyrical and incantatory poems pretty well too. Who would have thought it? Of course it's the applause that makes me do it, the rush of good feeling when the audience claps and calls out, and I can understand—what I never could imagine before—how theatrical people are stimulated and driven by this. It's a great feeling. But at the same time I don't like it. What does it have to do with poetry? I'd rather just be a poet, working in my little shack in the woods with no thought of all the hoopla out there.

Had a postcard from Jean and Adrienne in Ireland. It made me wish I were there. Or rather it made me wish I wished I were there. But I don't really. I like to think about being there but I have no real desire to go. I'm an armchair traveler if there ever was one, yet I don't read travel books. I read the atlas, sometimes for hours, imagining myself in different places, just as I imagine myself living in the houses I pass when I'm driving down the road at night. In fact imagining myself as someone else has been the most constant factor in my life from early childhood, I think, I've always done it, it is the perpetual substance of my daydreams. Is it like that with you? At any rate you did a remarkable job of getting inside another person in your Akhmatova translations.

It's a gray chilly day here, same as ever. Maybe the weather in Pennsylvania will be better.

Love, as always,

June 13, 1994

Dear Jane,

It's Saturday, about two in the afternoon, although I won't be able to print this until Monday when we're at home again, and then the computer will automatically update the letter. I'm in Wassergass, Pa., a very small community near Hellertown, which in turn is near Bethlehem; Wassergass is what would be called a settlement in Vermont, but I don't know what it's called here. There's a general store with a gas pump outside at the crossroad, and a church diagonally opposite, but that's all—no post office or town clerk or anything like that. The mailing address is Hellertown. I'm sitting in the living room of Len Roberts' old farmhouse, which he has restored and enlarged beautifully, doing all the work himself, and I can look out the window toward the slope that leads down to Len's pond, though in fact I can't see much of the pond because a big juniper hedge is in the way. I think if I lived here I might forego the hedge in favor of the pond and the birds that live and visit there. It's a magnificent frog pond with a full complement of bullfrogs in residence, and they make a lovely chorale at night. Last night after everyone else had gone to bed I sat and listened to the frogs for an hour and a half, completely enthralled. There were at least a dozen voices in a dozen different pitches, but all bullfrog voices down in the bass clef. They sang for 30 to 45 seconds at a time, then were silent for 15 to 20 seconds, then began again. Always one of the voices would begin with four low tones, followed by others in counterpoint and syncopation, until the whole band was going in a beautiful polyrhythmic structure, though the basic 4/4 beat was sustained throughout. Then when they stopped I would count the beats during their silence, and invariably they started up again in exactly the same time and rhythm; you could put a metronome on it. What I'm saying is that these guys are marvelous musicians, not at all simple or simple-minded. Each piece was different from all the others, a complex improvisation, yet keeping the beat exactly; I believe they kept that beat going all night long without ever losing it. I've heard other kinds of communal song from the animal world, wolf-song (a friend of Joe-Anne's in Arizona has forty-five wolves) and crow-call, the sounds of whales, etc., but never anything as beautifully unified within diversity as this. People say, oh, that's just a mating song or an assertion of territorial protectiveness, but though sex and territory were no doubt involved, as they are in all good art, I had no doubt whatever that the frogs were singing for pure joy in music. Nothing else could have sustained them for so long in their spontaneous inventiveness.

Earlier a number of people were here, local writers, Steve Berg and Bill Kulik from Philly, a small group. We drank wine and ate barbecue with all the fixings, and Steve brought a bottle of Remy Martin which we pretty well polished off afterward, watching the basketball playoff. It was a very pleasant occasion. Gerry Stern didn't come, as we had expected, because he has a broken rib, and I know how painful that is. He had a leg-cramp in the night, got up to walk it off, stumbled over something in the dark, fell and broke his rib: the kind of thing that happens. We sat outside in the shade of a big old sugar maple, enjoying the warm afternoon and then the cool breeze of evening. The night before I gave a reading and seminar at Lehigh University in Bethlehem (the home town of H.D.), and if I say so myself I was pretty spontaneously inventive also. The audience was a small but likable group of writers enrolled in a summer program there, people of all ages from undergraduates to grandparents. I was feeling ill because of my head and all the antibiotics, etc., but I read well and spoke well. I've noticed in the past that I give the best performances when I feel the worst, I don't know why.

We'll drive home tomorrow. Hope Stacey and the cats are okay.

Love,

June 21, 1994

Dear Jane,

Well, I've been a bad boy, not to say a wastrel and no-goodnik. I intended to write you a letter right after I had my supper, but I decided first I'd read a few poems in a new book by an acquaintance in South Dakota and write him a note; but after I'd read five poems I was so drowsy I went upstairs and lay on the bed and fell asleep for over an hour. Then when I woke I picked up the Bo's Nintendo game, the rudimentary hand-held kind with the little geometrical shapes that drift down, and I played the damned thing until Joe-Anne came home from Syracuse at 11:30. So now it's nearly midnight and I'm just beginning your letter. Forgive me.

I scored over 37,000 points at level 3, however, which I believe is my highest score ever.

By the time I print this it will be tomorrow, the Summer

Solstice, the time when the sun (Sol) stands still (sticere). Which makes this Midsummer's Eve. I believe Bottom is standing just outside my door, the man with the moon at both ends.

Myself, I'm sitting in my usual chair with the kitchen door open, a pleasant cooling breeze blowing in. Another advantage of the portable computer is that there's no paper to flap and sail off in the wind, no need for paperweights and curses. I sit here in my shorts and threadbare pale-green t-shirt with only this nicely compact apparatus to encumber me. Stacey is lying on my bare toes, a cozy arrangement. And there goes the clock. Happy Solstice! The clock, incidentally, is my only heirloom. After living with Don that must seem strange to you, how can there be such a paucity of mementos in a Yankee family? But the Carruths have been wanderers and unlucky at that. The clock was given to my mother and father for a wedding present in 1919. Since I was born in 1921 the clock has been a constant presence in nearly all my life, except for the time I was in the army and then living in Chicago. I wind it every Sunday night. It's only an ordinary Connecticut valley clock with a wooden case in the shape of a pointed arch, but it has a pleasant chime on the hours, not music, just the counting bell, which I like. The winding key turns stiffly, and at the end of his life my father couldn't wind the clock any more because of pain in his hands and wrists and he asked me to do it. Now I'm older than he was when he died and I can still wind the clock myself, which puts me one up on the old son-of-a-bitch, as I remark to myself with some small gratification every Sunday night.

Thanks for the postcard. But you needn't, you know. These letters of mine are written specifically NOT to be answered.

I hope you're holding up in this hot, sultry weather. I hope you have a good air conditioner for the room where you spend your time. If you don't please permit me to give you one.

Tomorrow I must go to Syracuse for an appointment with the surgeon to follow up on what he did for (to) me a couple of months ago. I believe the operation went well and so did my recovery. The only thing I'm anxious about is that he may tell me I must now have the same procedure again on the other side, my right carotid. I would not care for that, though if I must do it I'll manage. After I'm finished with him I'll pay a visit to a friend who is having the same trouble plus a bad heart attack, a painter and sculptor named Jack Nelson, whose work I like a lot. Like many graphic artists he has a fascinating house filled with all kinds of striking objects, both made and found, a big stone house, dim and cool inside, a good place to sit and drink a glass of wine on a hot summer day. I remember years ago visiting the home of Juan Gris—or was it Magritte? Christ, I can't remember—in Woodbury, Conn., after the artist had died. His widow was a friend of a friend. A restored 18th century saltbox house with small-paned windows and bar-latches on the doors. In the entrance hall was a billiard table with a hand in the middle of it (a glover's model actually) and in the hand rested a beautiful, many-colored porcelain egg. In another room was a whole wall covered with kachina dolls.

Woodbury was the town I lived in when I was a child, a poor farming community. After I left—naturally—it became a posh exurb for successful artists and their patrons. In 1935 my father sold the house we lived in there, another 18th century saltbox, for $4,000. Now it's probably worth $400,000.

Ah, me, how the years have flown! Which is a silly observation if there ever was one.

My dear, I think of you continually. I hope you can be

comfortable at least some of the time. Are you working? You shouldn't send me notes or cards, but if you have a new poem that you could send me a copy of I'd like very much to see it.

Love,

Ψ.

June 24, 1994

Dear Jane,

It's Friday, about noontime. The rain began at midnight last night and is still falling. It strummed on our metal roof all night, so that each time either of us woke up we could listen for a second or two, then move a half inch closer to the other in our creaturely warmth and complacency, knowing we were safe and dry. Knowing also that after weeks of hot weather the June drought is breaking, the cornfields are being drenched, our flowers won't need watering for a few days. Yesterday was hot and sunny. The first day lilies opened, their coarse, almost hungry blossoms reaching out to us. The apple trees are pruning themselves, scattering hundreds of little green apples, like marbles, on the ground. We've come to high summer. I think of afternoons on the river when I was a kid, or of evenings in the canoe in Maine, drifting on still water under the fuzzy stars. I do not think of stifling nights on the fire escape in Chicago. If I were Jim Wright instead of who I am, I'd probably remember the discomfort of the city, the squalor, the rats, which I knew at one time as intimately as he ever did, but I'm myself, I can't help it, I remember the good times—so irretrievably gone—and I'm not sure the pain of the one memory isn't as intense as that of the other. Meanwhile the rain falls beautifully. The murmur on the roof is musical and variable. I am in the bedroom so I can hear it, and Joe Anne has finally stumbled out of bed and gone to work. She'll be back in a couple of hours. We—all of us—are burdened by history, no doubt of that, but the burden is not so great that we can't respond to the same events when they recur in the present, the rain, the sunset, the opening of the day lilies. And I suppose that's a boon.

Teeth. I think about them almost continually. All my life I've been going to the dentist with frightening frequency, shelling out immense quantities of money that I didn't have. It's a matter of genes, I think. (Also a matter of psychosomatic tooth decay, though I've never been able to convince a dentist of that.) Lately my back molar on the lower left has begun to move, creating impaction with the tooth in front of it, which in turn creates pain throughout the left side of my head— sinus, ear, temple. My friend Stephen Dobyns believes that that rear molar, which sits about half an inch from the site of the incision when I had my operation a couple of months ago, was so frightened by what was happening next-door that it began to push in the opposite direction. I wouldn't be surprised. Did you ever read Defoe's *Journal of the Plague Year?* He quotes the weekly death lists for the city of London throughout the year—1665 I think it was—and of course the cause of death always given at the top of the list is the plague. But the second cause of death in many, many weeks was toothache. When I first read that I was struck by it forcibly, believe me. And I've never forgotten it. No wonder those people drank so much gin.

I got moderately drunk myself a week or so ago, when I was down in Pennsylvania, sitting under the shade of a big maple, drinking Courvoisier that Steve Berg brought me from Philadelphia. (He knows I like it.) I felt no pain. Teeth vanished, arthritic joints banished, all organs functioning smoothly and felicitously as they were intended to do. What could be better? Then the next day I felt—well, not as alert as one might wish, let's say. I don't wonder that the fundamentalists believe in an angry God.

Downstairs the radio is telling the story of David and Goliath, I don't know why. Even the public radio is becoming religious in these apocalyptic times. I can't hear it well enough to try to listen, but I hear some of it from time to time, the narrator's bland voice rehearsing the details of ancient violence. Now the story has ended and a "test of the emergency broadcast system" has begun, the high-pitched tone that might be signaling an atomic disaster. I wonder if the programmer at the station juxtaposed these two broadcasts deliberately?

I look out the window and see my neighbor's house a hundred feet away on this backcountry road that the natives call Hollywood Boulevard. I see a tractor, two motorcycles, a couple of snowmobiles, a pickup, three cars, all defunct and rusting, an unfinished deck that has rested as it is for three years, tall grass and weeds, a fat black and white cat nosing around for mice and moles, the animal and mineral detritus of civilization—and human. Here in our house we have books and poetry. Is there any difference? Not much. Maybe a little.

I look at the shelves next to me and see names like Catullus, Sartre, Delmore Schwartz, Hesse, Black Elk, Prescott, Trotsky, even Hayden Carruth.

Is this a somber letter? Because of the rain? Who knows? I love the rain. And do I love being somber? I wouldn't be surprised.

Good cheer to you nevertheless and much love,

S,

June 26, 1994

Dear Jane,

Feeding the dog her breakfast has become a pleasant ritual. I wash out her dish, dry it, put in the food, sprinkle brewer's yeast on top—against the fleas, but for her it's a delicacy as well—and give her fresh water, while she stands wagging her tail and making little eager noises in her throat. This morning, however, when I set her dishes on the floor she went and got her ball, and dropped it at my feet, the way she does when she wants to entice me into a game. "Stacey, you're a strange and foolish dog," I said. "You'd rather play than eat." But then I began to see that in fact she was trying to thank me in the only way she can. She "assumes" that if playing ball gives her so much pleasure it must give everyone else pleasure too. She wanted to do something for me in return for her breakfast, and she can't imagine that I find the ball boring as hell. Which casts a new light on our relationship. When I out of a sense of obligation play with her and throw the ball for her to fetch and worry, she thinks (perhaps) that she's entertaining me, fulfilling her appointed role. We are both creatures of duty. I'm not sure if I like that myself. But clearly she does.

Love,

S,

July 4, 1994

Dear Jane,

HAPPY INDEPENDENCE DAY! Though it's bloody little independence any of us have in this world as far as I can see. Another part of the American frontier fantasy, so piously bolstered by "that idiot Thoreau." On the other hand Wendell points out that my animosity toward the Concordian pencil-maker is all based on his first book, a juvenile product, and I should take into account his later works as well, including his "good works." No doubt Wendell is right.

It's a beautiful summer day here with sun, clear skies, clean air, temperature about 80°. A good day for the picnickers and softballers. Not much sign of the Fourth here, however. Last night a few local kids were firing off blanks in their daddies' six-shooters, but aside from that I heard no explosives. Philip Booth just called from Castine to ask how I am—he is very solicitous of me—and he says over there the Fourth is a big event with potato-sack races on the green, lots of hot dogs and lemonade, a procession through the town, etc. Tonight they'll have fireworks set off on a little island two or three hundred yards offshore in the bay, and everyone will turn out to watch. It sounds comfy to me. Also New-Englandish. In Upstate NY we have our fireworks at the mall or the casino.

Meanwhile my former wife, the Bo's mother, is here visiting him in his trailer up on the hill behind us. Our relationship, hers and mine, is altogether amicable and even affectionate, but at the same time there's always a little edginess in the atmosphere when two wives are occupying the same turf—or is that just my imagination? I remember the little passage in the

Cantos about Dorothy and Olga in the same apartment during the house-crunch of the war at Rapallo. Well, Rose-Marie and Joe-Anne are not in the same house, except for brief visits, so it's okay. Sometimes I do suspect a little tacit compact between them, however. A shared superiority. Namely with respect to my general character and personal habits. I wouldn't be surprised.

We have a new dog in the neighborhood, an ugly little beige-colored pug from one of the trailers on the way to the quarry. As soon as Stacey saw him she ran out and they began to play together, chasing each other, cavorting, making little yips and nips, nothing at all bellicose. Then they disappeared up the alley—which is what I call the road to the quarry—and Joe-Anne had to put on her sandals and go trudging after them. We are so afraid that Stacey will get onto the highway, which is almost as dangerous as the interstate here, although on her own Stacey seems to have good sense about it. She is afraid of the cars. I hope this doesn't mean we can't let her out any more except on a leash, which is a hell of a nuisance.

Now we are going to celebrate the Fourth with a bunch of bacon and eggs, very degenerate and bad. Then I'll watch the soccer match between the U.S. and Brazil. I find it a very dull game, in fact, and wonder how so many people in the world can be excited, not to say hysterically fanatical, about it. But to avoid working I'll watch anything.

Love to you,

July 8, 1994

Dear Jane,

Since I've nothing better to do than bare my soul and its
trivia, here is a journal entry I made this morning:

"On the walls of our bedroom, since the reconstruction
winter before last, are only two pictures: the photo of Joe-
Anne holding her newborn or nearly newborn baby (Adam),
the charcoal drawing of me when I was eight or nine made
by Max. The photo of J-A is a fine example of the Madonna-
and-child genre, showing the upper part of her body, naked,
her breast with its enormous aureole, the helpless infant held
against her shoulder; it's a good photograph, an admirable
portrait, no matter who is the woman in it, though of course
she is very recognizable and in part we both like it because
of this. The drawing of me has a few small flaws but hardly
noticeable at first; it's a three-quarter view and the ear is
not quite in the right plane, for instance. But I expect it is an
accurate enough representation of myself in that remote time.
Max was a competent artist. Both pictures were important to
us before we met, both have been displayed by us for years.
I think the drawing of me was on the wall in the cowshed at
Crows Mark during the whole time I lived there. But notice.
When I hung these two pictures after our bedroom had been
renovated a year and a half ago, I placed them side by side
on the wall overlooking the bed. I placed the picture of Joe-
Anne slightly higher than the picture of me. I did this without
thinking. But why does the picture of Joe-Anne show her at
age 24 (I think), and the other one show me when I was almost
twenty years younger than that? Actually I am thirty years

older than she. Why is she holding a child and in the picture I am a child? Why is her picture higher than mine? Taken as a symbolic arrangement, though a wholly unpremeditated one, this reveals things that I—perhaps both of us?—might not want revealed. But there the pictures are. And probably they're true enough.

I saw this only today, the hottest day so far of the current heat wave. I'm limp. Images of death by brain fever or internal combustion are not far off.

My uncle Max was a painter in the late impressionist style, a graduate of the Art Students' League, a social misfit who lived with us much of the time when I was young. His work was shown occasionally at small galleries, but he never was "successful," though I like some of his paintings a lot. I liked him too. In 1942 he was drafted; his birthday was one day before the official cut-off, i.e., he was 45 when he entered the army. He was sent to a basic training camp in Wisconsin in the winter, where he lived in a cardboard barracks and did his drill on a frozen field. It was more than he could take. He died a couple of months later.

So much for that.

Thanks for your card. I trust by now the bad effects of the recent course of treatment have worn off, if that's the right word—I'm sure it isn't. Hang on, my dear. We have need of thee.

Love,

July 13, 1994

Dear Jane,

It's a quarter to six on Tuesday afternoon, a pleasant hour, small cool breeze from the west, the Bo is mowing my lawn for me—a big job, it takes four to five hours, he won't do it all today—and I'm sitting outdoors in a rickety lawn chair in the shade of a maple tree, with Stacey lying near my feet and a glass of Irish whiskey by my side. I'm smoking a pipe I bought on 23rd Street in Manhattan in 1950 from a tobacconist named Albert Hartwich from Bavaria—see how my mind (anyone's) retains useless information for so long? Poor old Al, who had a cleft pallet, he is long since under the ground. As for the whiskey, this is unusual for me, at least at this time of day, but for several weeks I've been afflicted with pain in my head, at times very severe—it makes tears come to my eyes—and the dentist's explanation, namely, that my back teeth are moving and impacted because I grind my teeth at night, is unbelievable. In the first place I don't grind my teeth. By a rough estimate I've lived—I mean for periods of six months or more—with sixteen different women in the past 53 years and not one of them has ever said I grind my teeth. So unless I do it in some mysterious silent way I presume the dentist is wrong. In the second place even if I did why would that make my teeth move—at this time of life! On top of this today I made five phone calls and drove 20 miles in an attempt to get some codeine, with utter zilch as the result. Hence the whiskey. I swear the health care system in Moscow is INFINITELY better than the health care system in Oneida, New York. Believe me, if I were to reproduce here all the conversations I've had today in my head with dentists and doctors this letter would be so voluminous I couldn't afford to mail it. I'm sure you know what I mean.

The Bo just came too close to me with his (my) machine and filled up my whiskey glass with grass. Well, it's all vegetables, eh? Good for those wretched little cells in there. Maybe it'll stop their complaining—hah. Fat chance.

I just threw Stacey's ball for her and she disappeared inside the grape vine and was gone for a full minute and a half. Then she came bouncing triumphantly back with the ball in her mouth. The ball is, or was, a green tennis ball; it is now an abomination.

Stacey is not too swift when it comes to finding balls. But she is a whiz at catching flies-on-the-wing. Snap, snap—they're gone.

Some of the other shit the Bo put in my glass does not look so savory. Small dead exoskeletons, etc. But—vegetable, animal, what's the diff? I have a certain faith in metabolism if not much else.

Lately I've been rereading, revising, and typing essays from the 1970s when I was at the "height" of my "powers"—what garbage! And I thought I was defending good sense and good faith, if not civilization itself! I can hardly stand to put them down on paper again, such pompous rubbish. Yet I guess I must, I have a publishing contract to fulfill. And I know in my heart of hearts I should throw them into the incinerator. Wipe them out, get rid of them forever, save my successors the effort of doing it for me. How discouraging.

Well, the Bo snagged a rope (that had been used for tying Stacey) with the machine, and jerked the lawn chair next to me off its feet, spilling my whiskey, breaking the glass—though fortunately no damage to me or the computer. So much for rusticity. I'm back in the kitchen in my old chair, which I guess is rustic enough. Stacey is calming her alarm.

Love, as ever,

14 July 1994 (postcard)

Jane,
VIVE LA REPUBLIQUE!

July 18, 1994

Dear Jane,

A sluggish, listless time here. This is what I was thinking this morning, so I had to go look up "list" in the big dictionary, having in mind that the wind "bloweth where it listeth," my guess being that the root meaning had to do with will, probably because that is what I felt I lack these days. Close, but no cigar. It has more to do with wish, desire, velleity. I guess that's close enough; I have plenty of wishes but not much ambition to pursue them. It seems as if the weather has been even more repetitious than usual, every day overcast, warm, very humid. My hygrometer hovers between 80% and 90%. I wish I weren't such a slave to the climate, but I am, always have been, no doubt it's a genetic thing. When I was a boy I wanted to live on Baffin Island or in Greenland, and I still do. I think it would be great to be the best-known poet in Thule.

Well, yesterday I did what Don probably does every day, I turned out 26 pieces of mail and got rid of almost though of course not all my arrears of correspondence. Letters zipping off to places all over the world. Gives me a virtuous feeling, though it's all bullshit, as everyone knows. Having worked a good deal in a cow barn I understand that the cycling and recycling of bovine wastes—except that they're not wastes—is what keeps the enterprise going. When I think of the tons I've recycled, in the barn and at my desk, I am momentarily astonished. No wonder my back hurts.

I don't know if it has anything to do with being a writer, but I have to look up words pretty often—just to be sure. In the same way I have to look up places in the atlas. If I'm reading a book and the author mentions Sedona, Ariz., I'm compelled to get out the atlas and look up Sedona, and then spend fifteen minutes studying the rest of Arizona, even though I know perfectly well where Sedona is and have studied the map of Arizona 900 times in the past 60 years. It's a madness. No doubt deeply connected with all my other madnesses and not connected with writing at all. I have to see the words and map-shapes there on the page. One of the maddest people I've ever known, in or out of the hatch, was a lexicographer in Chicago who was making a concordance of the Greek scriptures, and who prayed loudly all the time for divine guidance in his search for roots and affinities. At the end of the day he'd look at his stacks of index cards, thousands of them, and mutter, "Not enough. Not enough." Then he'd look at me and say, "Hayden, the Lord was not with me today." Who knows what he did then? Probably went home and beat his wife if he had one. He was a little, dark guy, an Armenian from Smyrna.

The bee balm is gorgeous, three colors, dark red, medium,

and pink, a profusion. The hummingbirds love it. I try to track their flight when they depart, hoping to find their nest. But they zip off like bullets, across the road and into the thickets; in a hundred years I'd never find their nest, which I'm sure is copacetic with the hummingbirds. Once years ago when I had a little cabin on a small lake in Michigan they made their nest on my stoop, up under the eaves, and I could watch them easily—miniature domesticity like an animated doll-house. Actually they didn't seem to mind my presence at all. But elsewhere I've never known them to nest that boldly.

My first hollyhocks have bloomed and the sumac cones are turning red, not dark yet, but they look fresh and rosy. Our sumac grove is a nuisance, always encroaching on everything else, but at this time of year it is handsome, really quite spectacular if you can sever yourself from our natural anti-sumac prejudice for a while. I like to look at it. Once at a party a gushy fellow-guest said to G.B. Shaw: "Mr. Shaw, do you realize that 'sumac' and 'sugar' are the only words in English spelled with an 's' but pronounced 'sh'?" To which the great man replied: "Sure."

Love to you,

~~~

July 27, 1994

Dear Jane,

Seems like a long time since I've written. I apologize. I'm getting lazier and lazier as the summer progresses, no doubt of that. It reminds me of the long summers of my childhood in the 1920s, nothing to do day after day. Not that I was bored, not that I didn't have plenty of chores, both assigned and self-imposed. One of the latter was to go swimming every day no matter what, which entailed a 45-minute bike ride to and from the river. It was the Pomperaug River in western Connecticut, which eventually flows into the Housatonic. We swam at a place where an iron bridge crossed the river and the water was fairly deep and wide. The top framework of the bridge was about 30 feet above the water, and no boy was any good who wouldn't climb up there and dive off. The first time I did it I hit bottom and came up with my chest covered with blood, but it didn't deter me. I became a pretty good diver. Now I couldn't even stand on that high girder without a vertiginous disaster. It was a good swimming hole. We swam alongside the fish, snakes, turtles, water insects—including the dreaded giant water beetle—with neither fear nor repugnance, though we kept our eyes out for snappers. We used to say that if you killed a snake and buried it with the tip of its tail aboveground, the tail would "wiggle until sundown," and that was more or less true. Then at the end of the day there was the long slow ride home, past the blacksmith shop, where we always stopped. The blacksmith would heat his hammer in the forge, then spit on the anvil and hit the spit with the hot hammer, and it would make a report like a rifle shot. Mostly he was shoeing horses—I always admired the neat way he drove the nails through the hoof from the bottom and then filed off the nail-tips to make little silver ornaments on the top—but he did a lot of other things too. I had an 8x10 Meriden printing press and one time it fell off its cabinet and broke; the blacksmith brazed it together without using any torches. He was a clever guy.

Of course the main thing about swimming was seeing the girls, who had been bundled up all winter at school, in their bathing suits. Not bikinis, far from it, but still there was a fair amount of exposed skin. Most of the girls were just beginning to grow breasts; they had good-looking legs and neat little asses. All I ever did was look, of course, furtive and fascinated. Then just when I got to the age at which I might have thought about actually doing something, my family moved away, and I had to swim in the chlorine-stench of a municipal pool, under the eyes of lifeguards. The world was never the same again.

Not much swimming around Munnsville. Neither a swimming hole or a pool. I don't know what the kids do. Go ramming around in their illegal pickups probably, or on their rickety motorcycles, drinking beer and smoking dope, etc. We do have a creek in the bottom of the valley, but a small one, not much good for swimming. Here on our place we have no water at all, and I miss the brook that ran behind the house in Vermont. It was icy, too small for swimming. But at least you could jump in for ten seconds on a hot summer day and cool off. Once Fergus and I (that's Galway and Ines's boy) found a five-lined skink in the brook and Fergus took it home. Next time I was in Sheffield I asked him about it. "It died," Fergus said. Ted Hoagland was sitting there and said, "Oh that wasn't a skink, that was a salamander." He had never even laid eyes on the animal! A little while later he sold a piece to the NY Times Magazine in which he referred to New England farmers who can't tell a skink from a salamander. I've never forgotten that. I can goddamn well tell the difference between a skink and a salamander (which really don't look much alike), and I resent Ted's pigheadedness to this day. Now he's over there in

Bennington living the life of Riley in a big house —or at least he was the last time I heard from him. I remember sitting in his yard one time a couple of years ago with a well-fed python draped around my neck. Actually we're pretty good friends. When I remind him about the skink he shrugs it off.

Enough. Forgive me. In old age I get not only lazier and lazier but more and more prone to aimless garrulity.

Love,

August 6, 1994

Dear Jane,

Here I am in Wolcott, Vt., in David Budbill's cabin, one of the nicest places I know. In the woods, in a little, very green clearing among the spruces, hemlocks, and maples—the light in my windows is green—about eight miles from the highway, a quarter of a mile from David's house; it's easy to get to, but as quiet and isolated as one would care to be. It's now about 7:00 on Friday evening; I've been here by myself since 1:00 and now I'm waiting for David and Lois to return from Maine, where they've been vacationing, to see what we're going to do about dinner. If they don't come soon I'll drive over to Hardwick the nearest town, and eat by myself. Unfortunately I feel as bad physically as I ever have, so I can't completely enjoy being here. The drive over from Upstate NY was too much for me. My teeth—especially the ones that were pulled out earlier this week but all the others too—hurt terribly, with pain extending into my eyes, ears, sinuses, temples, etc.

43

My arthritic neck and shoulders are very sore. My stomach hurts, my heart is pounding. Etc. Aging is inexorable, but it isn't gradual, as younger people expect; it's a series of crises. And each one seems like death itself. Last night I stayed on the mountain east of Rutland in an adequate but dreary and noisy motel.

Meanwhile, as you of course know, the weather has changed dramatically—from stifling to chilly. I didn't bring the thick shirts and warm sweaters I should have. God knows I'm well enough acquainted with the climate of northern New England and I should have known better, but I reckon I was so fully acclimated to the steam and sweat that a change this immoderate didn't occur to me.

I'm here because I'm supposed to be writing an intro for a republication of some of Rowland Robinson's stories by the University Press of New England. It's a project I began 25 years ago. David is editing the text, and my intro will be a redaction of a monograph I wrote in 1972. But I left the bloody manuscript in Munnsville! Another crisis of aging—the loss of very perceptible chunks of my mind—and just as painful as the head and back, damn it.

I had my 73rd birthday two days ago. There's no disputing the numbers.

Well, I try to keep on as well as I can. No poems for quite a while now, but a fairly steady stream of other stuff. I'll have a selected essays next year and a new book of poems, i.e. things written since the *Collected,* the year after that. I usually work four or five hours a day. But I'm slow and lazy and reluctant, don't accomplish as much as I used to. Now I'm missing Joe-Anne and I wish she were here. She probably wouldn't care much for this cabin as a general thing, but for a few days she'd like it.

Have you watched or listened to any of the Whitewater hearings? A stupid business. Yet I have a capacity for getting caught up in such political dramas. The conflict of powers has something altogether Shakespearean about it, even if most of the language is outrageously deficient.

I hope you and Don are doing as well as you can. I'll send more news of the woods in a couple of days.

Love always,

8 August 1994

Dear Jane,

Well, I have a hangover—no point in disguising it. I got drunk at Galway's last night. I don't know how many bottles of wine we drank but David Budbill says he counted seven empties on the table and I know Galway was going down cellar damn regularly to get new ones. Bobbie, who seems as charming and intelligent as ever, and Lois, David's wife who has been my friend for many, many years, didn't drink much, and Lois was easily able to drive us home at midnight. What did we do—besides drinking? My memory is vague. We talked and disputed about everything and told lots of outrageous stories. We were behaving like kids in other words, which is probably not a bad idea from time to time. We had a hell of a good time, and I very much enjoyed seeing Galway again and being in Sheffield. It was a great day and we could see to New Hampshire clearly. In the afternoon the three of us read at the

Bread & Puppet Circus, but Galway and I left after the reading because we didn't feel up to the circus itself. I saw a few old friends there.

Galway read new poems including one written just a few days ago and I thought they were great.

So today I'm supposed to be working but I'm not. I'm not suffering greatly, and in fact all the wine seems to have been good for my aches and pains, which have diminished a little. But I'm not dancing on the clouds either. I'll work tomorrow. I went for a walk in the woods and found gentians in bloom, the beautiful peeping blue. Seems early. Everything seems early. We're eating fine tomatoes from David's garden. The corn is ripe.

Love,

[signature]

August 15, 1994

Dear Jane,

It's 3:00 AM, I can't sleep, my head is killing me, but at least I'm at home. Earlier than planned. I left Vermont at about noontime and drove all the way in one shot, a lovely drive through the mountains where I saw many signs of autumn, color in some of the maples, masses of goldenrod and asters on the roadsides—which seems early. But everything is early this year. Even in northern Vermont the tomatoes are already yielding heavily, very big and delicious fruit. It seems to me in the old days we never got any appreciable crop until the last week of August. And then the frost would come in the first week of September. I am full of pain and weakness and have been for some time, and the trip to Vermont was not at all a success—I think it will be my last. It's great to be at home with Joe-Anne again. But at least in Vermont I did the main thing I was supposed to do there, namely, finished a draft of a revised intro for the Robinson selection, cutting my original monograph from 80 pages to 50. I'm done with it. If they want anything more they can find someone else to do it.

Now people want me to give readings in Seattle, Portland, and Vancouver at the end of October, and I must commit myself within a day or two. I'm uncertain what to do. The audiences love me out there, and I know I can sell some books, but will I be up to it? Impossible question.

I'm sitting in the kitchen. We have a cricket somewhere, a cheerful little voice in the corner. I've been trying to remember "The Cricket on the Hearth," which I read when I was ten or eleven years old; but it's gone from me. The refrigerator is singing too, a little duet. Joe-Anne is asleep upstairs, having taken a pill, and perhaps that's what I should do too, though I've been doing my best to cut back on the medications. Why? What difference does it make? None probably, except that they're damnably expensive. Also I have to get the Dalmane semi-illegally because the doctors around here refuse to prescribe it for me.

Well, my dear, I hope you are asleep and having a nice dream. The other night I dreamt that someone gave me a book entitled *Ready, Set, Fuck You*—which made me laugh. Laughing dreams are the best.

Love,

For Jane,
  A Sampler

LET THE SUN SHINE ON
YOU, OR THE SILVER RAIN,
TO SOOTHEN, OR TO WASH
AWAY, YOUR PAIN.

August 23, 1994

Dear Jane,

I'm sorry it's been so long since I wrote last. We've been having a minor crisis here. I've had bad pain in my head for quite a while—it spoiled my trip to Vermont and I came home sooner than expected—and then a few days ago it reached such a pitch that I went to the emergency room in Oneida, where a likable young doctor ordered CAT scans for my brain and sinus. The result is that I have a possible aneurysm in my brain and must have an MRI exam tomorrow in Syracuse to get a clearer picture. A nuisance, to say the least. It seems as if I've been in the hands of the doctors continually for the past year, and I know you of all people understand what that means.

I've been sending out form letters in an effort to cut off—or cut down—the inflow of books, mss., letters, etc., and I've quit answering the phone.

Meanwhile we're having a splendid day here, sunny, clear, temperature about 75°, the kind of summer day one always hopes for but seldom gets. I will try to do a little work outside this afternoon, pulling up the dead stalks of the day lilies, for instance. Or trimming the wretched box elder that got damaged in a storm last week. Joe-Anne has gone to the dentist. She hasn't been feeling well lately, a consequence of too much stress, I think. Nothing serious. Last night I talked on the phone with Adrienne and we spoke of you admiringly and affectionately. You are a peach, in case you didn't know.

Love,

August 27, 1994

Dear Jane,

There was joy in this house last night, probably a little too much. I learned yesterday afternoon that the Damoclean sword I'd been living under for a week, namely, the possibility of an aneurysm in my brain, has been removed: the MRI exam showed a "normal" brain. All my dire fantasies were dispelled at a stroke, and Joe-Anne's too. She had been feeling the stress; stomach upset and so on. She went shopping late in the day and bought a bottle of champagne that we had with our dinner and then afterward we started in on a jug of plonk. We played music and danced and talked endlessly, etc.

Well, the pain is still there though improved by high-powered painkillers and antibiotics. The cause is still obscure. We'll see what happens. But for the time being we have a respite. The little crisis has passed. The next one is no doubt being born somewhere right now, like Yeats's brute, and will be slouching toward Munnsville before long. That's life, as they say.

I wish—we both wish, so fervently—we could bring about

a respite for you too. You must be reading these words with a good deal of bitterness, which is natural and right. And of course the thought occurs to me that I shouldn't be sending you this news, that I should edit and trim my words to suit your circumstances. But I find I can't, I am unable to place myself in relationship with you in anything less than full human candor and sincerity, as well as love, because that is the kind of person you are. It is clear in your poems. It is clear in everything I know about you.

Otherwise things here are quiet and uneventful. Our poor dog Stacey has had to spend the night at the vet's because of an infection and allergy, a problem that seems to be perpetual with her. She'll come home today. Joe-Anne has been reading Don's *Museum*, and that's one of the things we talked about last night. She is contemplating a low-level teaching job—technical writing—at a local college in Utica, and we talked about that too. I don't want her to take a full-time job unless she desires it for nonfinancial reasons, as long as we can get along on my income at any rate. On the other hand she is going to need to earn at least part of her own living after I'm gone, so it might be a good idea to make an institutional connection now, although neither of us is much persuaded by that argument. She is writing, doing good work, and I think that's what she should continue to do.

I spoke with Adrienne on the phone yesterday and she seems to be in good shape. She says she is. She is writing. For once the MacArthur foundation did exactly the right thing, I believe, and I was extremely pleased by the news.

A whole bunch of wretched little flies has invaded our house in the past week or so, doubtless a new seasonal species.

Pesky. I don't know how they get in, though in an old house like this there must be hundreds of ways. Stacey catches them—snap, snap—when she can. And I go stalking with the fly swatter, not very effectively. Also we have some rats living under our stoop, brown rats, Norway rats; I see them scurrying about when I turn on the outdoor light suddenly at night. We don't mind them. They eat the sunflower seeds from the bird-feeder. The coons come snarling around at night too. Day before yesterday I saw a great heron standing at the edge of a small pond on a farm up in the hills, a perfect hieroglyph. The trees we planted, a tulip poplar and white birch, seem to be doing well. But the place looks generally ragged and neglected, as it is.

I have been reading nothing but novels of crime and espionage, drug-store books, what we used to call "cheap-screw fiction." And I can't remember most of the time what was on the previous page as I'm reading. It doesn't matter any more. Reading is not for information but for the flow of language and the old associations in my head.

Much love,

August 31, 1994

Dear Jane,

We are appalled by the news of your mother's illness. Such a burden of misery you people are carrying. As you say, it isn't fair—not that fairness appears to have much to do with human events one way or another. But it would be comforting if we could come up with some kind of rationale for mere, brutal misfortune, aside from God's superior wisdom, in which I personally haven't much faith or interest. I suspect—but I certainly don't know—that the great increase in cancer and other illnesses of the immune system is our own fault somehow, the result of pollution, moral and material. At all events I hope your mother can be as comfortable as her predicament will permit, and that you somehow are finding the fortitude to deal with all this. You must be sure to tell us if there's anything we can do.

The last day of August here is, appropriately, rather chilly and gray. I look out my window at the sumac grove and the cones are bright red, quite pretty. The mountain ash here and there are bright with their orange berries, and I've decided the next tree I plant will be one of them. The English call them rowan trees. In northern Vermont I transplanted one from the woods to my yard and it took well, but around here mountain ash does not grow wild, I'll have to buy one. The robins and flickers are gone, also the orioles and redwings—early, it seems—and everyone is predicting another long, hard winter. I don't know what the woolly bears are saying; I haven't seen one yet. Maybe they've given up in disgust.

Poor Stacey has a bad ear, combination of infection and allergy apparently, she's been overnight to the vet, very expensive, and now we must put medicine in her ear. But she won't let us. Astonishing how strong a terrified animal can be. The Bo and I tried together to hold her still, but we couldn't. Now we're trying a tranquilizer prescribed by the vet. According to our pharmacology book it's a variant of Thorazine, which I lived on for many years though it never did me much good. Joe-Anne gave her the tranquilizer about twenty minutes ago, but Stacey still isn't relaxed enough to let us administer the medicine, and I wonder if she will. Drugs, medicines, we are ruled by them. Reminds me of your poem.

Love to you both,

$\wp$,

September 8, 1994

Dear Jane,

I'm sitting here in my customary kitchen chair watching this mushroom grow before my eyes. Or some kind of fungus, I don't know what. It's growing between the bricks that make the footing for our woodstove. Very peculiar. I don't believe I've ever had a mushroom growing in my house before, not counting the cellar. It is white and bulbous and multiform, with many interleaving parts, a little obscene, as a matter of fact, like a cluster of vulvae on my kitchen floor—or is that just my outré imagination? But mainly it is growing fast, so fast that when I say I'm watching it grow I hardly exaggerate. It has doubled in size since this morning. (I'm writing in mid-afternoon, another splendid day, sunny but cool. I've just watered my birch and tulip poplar saplings, which are doing well.) I can't say the mushroom is beautiful exactly, but it is interesting, a lot more interesting than any number of abstract paintings I've looked at, God knows. It strikes me that if one could sufficiently cultivate different kinds of mushrooms on one's floors and walls, one could have a continuous art-show-in-progress for one's décor. Not a bad idea.

Today's mail brings a letter from Don, dictated in the hospital last week. I'm sorry of course to learn you are continuing to have so much trouble with the chemo. It is dreadful, I know. I've had other friends who struggled with it, as we all have now—friends, I mean—and all one can really say is that it is necessary and often very helpful in the long run. It has saved my daughter Martha. The mail also brought letters from Jim Harrison, whose work (some of it) I like a good deal, and Adrienne, who enclosed the manuscript of her new book of poems. I'm eager to read it. She and Michelle are having a little vacation at Point Reyes, and I'm glad for them. Jim Harrison lives part of the time in the mountains on the Mexican border where New Mexico, Arizona, and Old Mexico came together, the same region in which Cormac McCarthy's new novel is located, called *The Crossing*. I've begun reading it. McCarthy is a remarkable writer, but I find something missing in his work: too much surface and not enough depth or resonance though I'd be hard-pressed to define those terms or defend that judgment in public. I like his book titled *Suttree* the best of what he's done so far.

Joe-Anne is in New Jersey. She's fine. I bought her a laptop computer to take with her. Myself, I'm driving over to Vermont tomorrow to give a reading at a bookstore in Manchester Center, arranged by the publisher. If I don't get sidetracked I'll come back the next day. I look forward to the drive. We have color now in our roadside maples, lots of goldenrod and asters, and I'm sure I could find gentian, ladies tresses, turtlehead, etc., if I knew where to look for them. I used to know when I lived in Vermont, but I don't know here. So many things have changed. The ground here is littered with

pears and apples, which distresses me, it's such a waste, but I
no longer have any ambition to gather them or eat them. So
they rot in the grass. The bees and yellowjackets love it, the
deer also. A lot to tipsiness and revelry around there, in fact. I
eat peanut butter. And drink a little Irish whiskey for the sake
of my soul.

With Love,

September 10, 1994

Dear Jane,

It's Friday afternoon, September 9th, about 4:30, and I'm
in Manchester Center, Vt., in a very posh motel, for which I'm
sure Copper Canyon is spending far too much money—the
kind of thing I really disapprove of. It makes me angry; it's
wasteful and unnecessary. Yet it has become built into the
consciousness of poets and other subsidized people as if it
were their right, the perks of being an homme d'esprit if not
an enfant terrible. It goes along with the whole inflationary
impetus of the American economy, based on credit, on
expense accounts, etc., based in other words on money spent
unproductively. Well, at the same time it's comfortable. The
motel consists of about a dozen small buildings on a hillside
north of town, looking out toward the west, toward Mt.
Equinox and the other Taconic Mountains, with the Green
Mountains at our back. (Most people, even natives, don't
know the distinction. I don't know how many poems I've read
that were written at Yaddo and make sentimental references to

the Green Mountains in the west, whereas from Saratoga you can't see the Green Mountains at all but only the Taconics.) My room is large, with two king-sized beds—who will share them with me?—and all the luxurious accouterments, including a balcony looking out over ten or twenty acres of well-mown, well-fertilized greensward. It's another fine September day, warm enough for me to sit out here in my t-shirt, but with a nice refreshing breeze, blue sky, interesting clouds, etc. So why do I complain? Because I'm a fucking lousy complainer since the moment my genes connected 74 years ago in an old iron bedstead on Central Ave. in Waterbury, Conn. That's why.

The drive over here took only four and a half hours, so I've plenty of time. I'm to have dinner with some people from the bookshop, which is as posh as the motel, at six, then read at seven-thirty. I will have to watch my mouth. Some sarcastic remark about gentrification is almost bound to slip out. Even though the topography is right, this doesn't even look like Vermont. Not a cow in sight, not a single shack held together with staples and masonite. Where are my people? The ones who used to go to Canada automatically at age 18 and get all their teeth pulled out, a standard rite of passage. The ones who believe you can't be an alcoholic if you drink nothing but beer. The ones who know how to roast a haunch of venison with onions and garlic and sage and mustard (and where to find the haunch in July). The ones who buy their clothes at the rummage and their cars at the junkyard. The ones who used to be me. Here I am on my balcony with a finger or two of cognac, a cigar, and a laptop computer, wearing my black jeans and my Reeboks. God, it's awful.

Well, I wish you and Don were here with me. We could

inject a little common sense, or at least commonness, into this scene.

Tell Don that major league ball is finished in America, and a damned good thing too. What a spectacle. Tell him he must get interested in the Concord Cougars or the Dublin Dodgers or whoever your local team may be. Myself, I root for the Utica Blue Sox.

I won't be able to print this out until I get home, probably won't be able to mail it until Monday. But you'll get it eventually.

With love, as always,

P.S. Next day. Home again. The drive was easy except that I have a tendency to fall asleep at the wheel. Not good. Pretty soon I'll have to disqualify myself from driving alone for more than an hour or so at a time. I stopped for lunch in Gloversville, N.Y., and ran into a bartender who was 83 years old and still on the job. As it happened the paper today in Amsterdam had a story about him with his picture, how he has worked in California and Arizona and Nevada and knows many famous people. He showed it to me proudly and we had a modest celebration. The reading last night went very well but we didn't sell many books. I think everyone in Vermont who is interested in my books already owns them.

The "mushroom" is now a foot in diameter and about four or five inches high. Quite a phenomenon. Like something out of a movie about aliens. I like to think it comes from outer space.

September 12, 1994

Dear Jane,

The "mushroom," which is fantastically big now, many-petaled, like some dream flower by Georgia O'Keefe, has matured. When I came in last night the floor around it was covered with fine white dust. This morning the dust is even more plentiful. It can only be spores, as far as I can see. And it's true that the "plant" is like a mushroom because it has thousands of gills, which I hadn't noticed at first. What it resembles most is the kind of shelf-fungus you find growing on dead trees, the kind you can write on with a stick. However, instead of a single shelf, this has many. I expect it is growing from old wood-dust and little splinters that have settled over the years into the cracks between the bricks. I'm supposed to be allergic to mold spores and penicillin and things like that, so I'll get rid of the spores, but I'm loath to get rid of the mushroom itself because it is so extraordinary. I wonder how long it continues emitting the spores?

A lonely old man in the morning will make friends with practically anything.

Love,

September 14, 1994

Dear Jane,

The episode of the "mushroom" has come to an end, and like most episodes of life the end has been less agreeable than the beginning and the middle. Night before last I damned near died from being unable to breathe. Gasping, wheezing, coughing, heaving, huffing. Since I am who I am I didn't call for help, but took a dose of Robitussin, a Dalmane, and a shot of cognac, and went to bed. I woke in the morning, feeling grateful but still asthmatic, so I hastened to get rid of the fungus, regretfully, it really was magnificent, an indubitable addition to the domestic landscape—but now it reposes on the compost pile, though I doubt if it will add much to the compost. The whole area where it had been was covered with a white residue, the spore dispersion, which I thought would be easy to remove, but when I tried the vacuum on it I found it was not dry, as I had expected, but moist and sticky. So I sprayed the whole region with Lysol and after twenty minutes cleaned it up with hot water and a sponge. In fact the bricks looked so clean and pristine that I went on and cleaned the stove and put blacking on it, which I had neglected to do last spring.

Now the question is: will the mushroom return? I know from my experience in the woods that most wood fungi have long, filament-like roots. In the case of the Dutch elm blight it's the roots that kill the tree, not the flower of the fungus. I'll be watching to see what happens.

That same day my cousin Olive and her husband came to see me. They were passing through. They live in California.

The last time I saw Olive she was about ten years old and I was in my mid-20s, a long time ago. Now she is 60 or so, a trim, good-looking woman with dyed blonde hair, a dark-browed Hungarian husband, a bright intelligent manner. Strange. I felt no sense of kinship whatever. Bloodlines mean nothing. I was closer to the mushroom.

Love,

September 22, 1994

Dear Jane,

I've been going to the dental clinic every day lately with massive doses of Novocain and antibiotics, so I haven't been writing many letters or doing much of anything else either. The technologists discovered a lot of hidden damage in my teeth that apparently accounts for the huge headaches; hidden because it was under the crowns that were put on my teeth years ago (crowns impenetrable to x-rays), damage because I had cracked the crowns or worn little holes in them that weren't at first evident. They tell me I am very hard on my teeth; they tell me I'm a tooth-grinder in my sleep. When I tell them that I've had four wives and a number of other acquaintances and none has ever complained, the clinicians look at me askance. I know what the problem is. The Carruth family have been notable trenchermen for generations with extraordinary development of jaw muscle. I remember my father who held the fork in his left hand, the knife in his right, as older people often did, and he used the knife to build up a forkful in a positively artistic way, patting it on the sides and top until he had as much as the fork could hold, all compact and tidy. Then he would ram it into his mouth as if he were plugging a leak in a dike. Whereupon would begin the most extraordinary chomping you can imagine, rippling jaw action, sliding and slithering at the temples, dancing ears. And the man had practically no trouble with his teeth as long as he lived. Well, I inherited my mother's fragile teeth and my father's robust table behavior, and the combination has been devastating all my life. Up in the North Country it used to be a rite of passage for young people when they turned eighteen to go to Canada and have all their teeth pulled out and replaced by false teeth. I knew many of them, including many old people. False teeth are a problem, but I think those people had less pain and spent a hell of a lot less money than I have. Even when I was poorest I always went to the dentist and somehow scrounged up the money to pay him, all because my genteel mother told me when I was a child that false teeth were a sign of lower-class sloth and degeneracy. What nonsense!

Anyway the pain has diminished and one of these days—or weeks or months—I'm told the dental reconstructions will be completed and I can go back to worrying about my arthritis and how to get downstairs in the morning.

Happy Equinox! This morning it's rather hazy outside, but the past few days have been wonderful, clear, bright, cool, the best September weather and extremely unusual in Upstate New York. The trees are turning, the asters—both New England and New York asters—are brilliant. My friend Ted Enslin of Maine used to make wine from aster blossoms, and it wasn't bad at all. Ted used to do a lot of other peculiar things too, for that matter, including the composition of an endless poem in many volumes that no one could read. But he owned an old abandoned farm in the middle of the woods in central Maine, and sometimes I used to go there on retreat. The house was falling down, but the kitchen was still intact and had a workable wood-range for warmth and coffee. Otherwise I lived on peanut butter and crackers. One night I woke up on the cot next to the kitchen window and looked out at the sky, which was brilliant with stars. I saw a comet. I could scarcely believe it, but the appearance was unmistakable, a bright forepart and a fan-shaped tail. The next morning I went ten miles to buy a copy of the *New York Times,* and sure enough, there was a little story on an inside page about a minor comet that had been visible the night before. I never saw another. All the famous ones which have caused so much excitement in the press over the years have been fizzles—either hidden by bad weather or totally unspectacular. I loved that place of Ted's. (He lived most of the time in the village in a much better house.) I saw bear and moose there, and a splendid variety of other wildlife, including eagles and northern shrikes. A brook flowed nearby. It was so far away from everything that you couldn't hear a single man-made noise ever, except sometimes the flickering of the oil lamp. But there was never a shortage of other things to listen to.

Now it's gone. Ted sold everything and moved over to the coast. I haven't heard from him in years.

I believe you'll be departing soon for Seattle, if you haven't already. I don't have Don's letter handy. Good luck out there. Please ask Don to keep me informed—VERY BRIEFLY–A POST-CARD IS ALL I NEED—of your whereabouts and how you are faring. I'll be in Seattle myself during the last week of October, and perhaps if you're up to it we could have a visit. I'll be reachable out there c/o Copper Canyon Press, P. O. Box 271, Port Townsend, WA 98368. Phone: 206-385-4925.

With much love, as ever,

September 26, 1994

Dear Jane,

Monday morning again here. Sometimes it seems as if the Monday mornings succeed each other at about ten-minute intervals. It's warm, temperature about 64°, and wet—not a hard rain but a steady drizzle that makes the maple leaves shine and the passing cars sing on the pavement. The animals have been fed and watered, the dog is curled at my feet, the cat is stretched out on the back of my chair, purring contentedly. So all's well. I'm up early, at least for me—I came downstairs at 9:00. Joe-Anne is still sleeping. I think it was past dawn when she came to bed last night. When I was her age I used to work all night often; in fact usually, so I know how it is, the urge to keep going, to finish, to clear the decks—a futile urge, of course. But now I can't do it; I get too tired and usually go to bed at about 2:00 or 3:00. A strange schedule we keep, most people would think so. If we want to spend time in bed together we have to make an appointment. "How about after dinner, around nine o'clock?" "Okay." Then after we've made love and snuggled and been friendly for a while, we get up and dress and go back to our separate workrooms. Sometimes if the night is clear the dog and I go out for a little walk around the meadow to look at the stars and listen for the screech owls up in the woods. Then I come back and write letters for a while and read for a while, and have something to eat, maybe a glass of wine if there is any, and gradually make my way to bed. At present I'm reading John le Carré's most recent spy novel; he's a good writer, though not brilliant, and almost succeeds in making his fantastic stories believable. Before this I read Cormac McCarthy's *The Crossing.* McCarthy may be a brilliant writer, I think he is at his best, but this new book has so much Spanish in it, a language I don't know except by inference from Latin and French, that I found it tedious and oppressive in large parts. I even gave up on it at one point and put it aside, and then later went back to it and finished it. Obviously it's possible to write a bilingual book in a predominantly monolingual culture, but I wonder if it's feasible. I've been thinking about this. It raises a good many questions, and maybe I'll write an essay about it though probably I won't. I've written enough essays, in fact far too many.

Well, I hope one way or another you're rested today, able to enjoy the rain on your windowpane. I know you must be taking a lot of painkillers and sedatives, etc. Myself, I love morphine and could easily become addicted to it, like the lotophagoi in Homer's story. Lying around in bliss while the sun shines and sea-fowl cavort, what could be better? But of course I'm such an up-country puritan at heart I'd suffer terribly from guilt and shame, and that would spoil everything.

The dog just began barking furiously, no doubt waking Joe-Anne because some workmen outside are doing something by the road. I chided her, the dog, and she looked at me reproachfully, and of course I don't want her to stop barking at strangers because that's one of the advantages of having her, so we're at an impasse without a conflict—Stacey and Joe-Anne and I. Which seems to be the primary condition of life. Joe-Anne could go back to sleep after an earthquake, so I'm not greatly concerned for her now. On the other hand she won't go to Seattle with me because she's afraid of airplanes. For that matter I'm afraid of them too, but I have to go.

Much love,

𝒫,

October 6, 1994

Dear Jane,

I'm sitting here contemplating my hibiscus. Last night I brought it in from its summer place on the stoop, with the Bo's help. It takes up a good part of this end of the kitchen and reaches to the ceiling. Five years ago it was a six-inch seedling in a pot from the supermarket that Joe-Anne bought for me, and I can't take much credit for what it has achieved in the meantime; I've watered and trimmed it and occasionally fertilized it, and that's about all. And now, unfortunately, I must take discredit for leaving it out too long, so that some of the foliage is brown and frost-bitten, although it has several splendid blossoms on it. Do you have experience with hibisci (if that's the right plural)? I could use some advice now. It needs to be cut back before I can fit it into its winter space in my workroom, where it towers over my desk. I've done this before but only gingerly. This year it needs major reshaping and reduction. It hurts me to cut the limbs because they all have flower-buds at the ends and I hate to lose them because normally the hibiscus blooms all winter as well as all summer, never more than three or four flowers at a time but never more than a few days without flowers either. I've read that in Asia some varieties grow sixty feet tall and have many blooms, which would be something worth seeing.

So I suppose I'll just get out the pruning shears and go clipping away ignorantly and hope that nature will make up for my deficiencies. She usually does.

Not much to report otherwise. Yesterday the Bo and I drove up onto the Tug Hill plateau north of here, which is the most unspoiled wilderness in New York State—and that's not saying much. It has been logged unsparingly; we saw almost no old-growth forest. But still the fall colors were bright, many parts of the plateau are completely uninhabited, at least by human beings. Around the edges are small farms, rather desolate—the weather is fierce up there in winter—the remnants of the self-sufficient farms established 100 years or more ago by settlers from who knows where. It's my kind of country: bleak, slashed, windblown, remote, rather ugly. Dirt roads and lots of mudholes even at this time of year. But I'd live up there if I could. The trouble is that I couldn't get anyone else to live with me, and probably I could no longer handle the practical arrangements by myself. Lots of water up there, ponds, brooks, one fair-sized river. Must be some kind of artesian effect underneath that forces the water up. We saw herons and loons and kingfishers. A number of big beaver dams. A good deal of red maple, some ash, hornbeam, etc., and plenty of black spruce, hemlock, tamarack, white pine. Bright purple asters everywhere.

Then the radiator hose in the Bo's old Grand Am sprung a leak. We were lucky to get to Lowville without breaking down, lucky to find someone who could replace the damaged hose. We had dinner at Lloyds of Lowville, the local diner. We had a drink in the North Country Saloon. Everyone up there, men, women, and children, wears a greasy old hat with John Deere written on it, or Purina Chow, or something like that. A great place.

Otherwise not much to report Joe-Anne has been seriously down in the dumps because her work isn't being published, and that affects all of us. A few days ago she trashed thirty poems in her computer—they are gone forever. She has made an appointment to see a recommended shrink in Syracuse and our local doctor has started her on Zoloft, and I hope this will help. Thirty poems is for her at least two years of work, probably three. What would help most would be getting out a book. She sits here in this house surrounded by thousands of books of poetry, many of which contain work not as good as hers, and this would be enough, aside from her innate predisposition toward despondency and self-distrust, to depress anybody.

Now I must get to the hibiscus.

Love ever,

October 16, 1994

Dear Jane,

Here it is, Sunday morning again, a bright autumn morning, and I've been remiss in my letter-writing lately, in part because my computer has been on the fritz and had to spend a week in the computer hospital in Utica, in part because I've been tied up with a lot of little chintzy chores, in part because my old body won't do what it's supposed to any more, or if it does it takes ten times longer than it used to. My left arm is nearly kaput. Fortunately it doesn't affect my hands much, except on the worst damp days, so I can still run the computer and drive the car. When I can no longer perform those operations I'll be in a hell of a shape.

Joe-Anne just came down—she always sleeps a couple of hours longer than I do—with her copious hair tousled, her nightgown rumpled and twisted, yawning and stretching. Last night we had dinner with Isabel and Stephen Dobyns in Syracuse, got home at about 1:00 AM, both of us with headaches and stomachaches, and we hadn't drunk enough to explain these symptoms. Stephen had cooked tuna steaks for our dinner, and Joe-Anne says, "Probably the tuna had mercury in it." She reads the science section of the *New York Times* religiously every week. Myself, I'm inclined to suspect the wine. Stephen has discovered an Australian wine called "Long Flat Red," which he likes because of its name, and in fact it tastes all right to me, nothing extraordinary but okay. Still who knows what those Aussies put in it? Kangaroo piss maybe.

Joe-Anne is on Zoloft now and is seeing a shrinker in Syracuse once a week, a guy who teaches not only in the medical school but also in the philosophy department, so he can't be all bad. She seems to be feeling cheerfuler. Not so much because the therapy has taken effect, I imagine, as because something is happening at last, a new phase of experience has begun. We hope for the best.

The reason my computer was in the shop, according to what the repairman wrote on the sales slip, was "excessive cat hair." "Do you have a white long-haired cat?" he asked. Indeed we do. Name of Smudgie, as I think I've mentioned before. She is a champion hair-producer, the stuff is all over the place, if we could only find a way to spin it we could make sweaters for all our friends, very fine sweaters. How the hair got into my computer is a little hard to understand because there doesn't appear to be a suitable entry point anywhere, but I'm not disputing the diagnosis: Smudgie's hair is everywhere. She's a good cat. The repairman suggested I get rid of her, but I said immediately, "Oh, I can't do that," implying that my wife wouldn't stand for it, which was a cowardly way out, and no doubt sexist too. The fact is I wouldn't stand for it either. The other afternoon I was sitting in the living room and Joe-Anne was in the kitchen, both of us listening to the news on NPR, when I heard this loud unaccountable banging and thumping from overhead. It sounded as if thieves had broken in. We went upstairs and there in Joe-Anne's workroom was Smudgie with her head stuck in a Kleenex box. She couldn't get it off. She was ramming around violently and of course blindly. I had to break the box myself to get it off her. "Silly," I said, "why did you stick your head in there?" Smudgie looked at me complacently and said, "None of your goddamned business."

Who can argue with that?

You mustn't suspect that if I don't write for a week I've forgotten about you. I think of you, we both do, all the time.

With much love, as always,

𝔤,

October 19, 1994

Dear Jane,

I woke up sneezing. An hour ago. Tickles and sniffles in my little schnoz. Odious. No doubt it occurs hundreds of thousands of times every day in the general population, the onset of the common cold, so perturbingly recognizable. People everywhere cursing the day with heartfelt fervor. One can almost feel the weight of all those maledictions settling to the ground in Illinois and Pennsylvania and Texas.

I have to leave for Seattle in a few days and I remember what happened last fall when I was there, so I'm apprehensive about this sneezing and what it may lead to. Nothing to do about it. Maybe there is; maybe I should investigate some of these patent cold medicines I see advertised so often. I've always been inclined to let nature take her course, but perhaps the time has come to intervene, if possible. I'll see what Joe-Anne says. She knows all about such things.

I wish she were going with me to Seattle. She declines, on the grounds that the flight would be too hard for her, which I don't doubt for a minute. She is not only afraid of flying, she is obsessed with accounts of disaster, and she can recite all the statistics and other pertinent data on famous crashes including the recent one in Pittsburgh or wherever it was.

So I'll go alone and she'll stay in Munnsville and take care of the animals.

Meanwhile, after a stretch of beautiful autumn weather, which I know extended to New Hampshire too, this is our second overcast and showery day, but warm—temperature in the high 50's already. It may get to 70° this afternoon. Maybe I'll rake some leaves, though it's too soon to do it seriously. The leaves on our trees have changed color but most of them haven't yet fallen. When I drive to town—Oneida—I see people along the way working in their yards, raking, trimming, hauling stuff in barrows, etc., and I feel guilty because I don't do as much as I should, as much as I used to, of that sort of work.

Yesterday I transplanted part of a lobelia to bring it in for the winter. I've kept it going for about five years. I love that brilliant blue, those delicate little blossoms. Each spring and fall I have to divide it and throw part of it away because it increases so vigorously; but it blooms summer and winter, it keeps going marvelously. Probably it's a weed. In fact it looks somewhat like chickweed except for the color.

Trivial pursuits. I should be writing a poem. But I don't have any ideas. Last night I revised my essay on Don's work, in which yours is also applauded—such wonderful poems—and transferred it to the manuscript for the *Selected Essays*. I thought of the nice visit I had with you that summer, though now I can't be sure which summer it was. 1988? I think that was the time when you and I drove to the nearby town where you do your shopping—I can never remember its name—and you were somewhat high on a new antidepressant, and we talked animatedly about all the different drugs we had taken, laughing at ourselves. It was a fine occasion, and it sticks in my mind. My manuscript is much too big, well over 600 pages now in the computer, so I'm not sure this essay will make it into the final book. I resist making decisions about things like that, I prefer to leave it up to Sam Hamill—although, to tell the truth, I'm not sure I trust anyone's judgment as well as my own, for that matter. But the emotional strain of making decisions is often too much for me.

Summer is over, no doubt of that. It was not a great summer for me or for most of my friends. Yet I miss the thrush-song, the flash of the orioles in the sycamore. Should I write a poem about that? Is there any possible way to write such a poem that I haven't used already, or that thousands of other poets haven't used? I suppose the only way to find out is to do it. Take a deep breath and begin. I'll let you know if anything comes of this.

With love, as ever,

ᵍ,

November 6, 1994

Dear Jane,

Again I've let a week go by without writing and I'm distressed about that. I've thought of you often, have wondered where you are and how you are faring. I've reached out a hand in my mind to touch your hand, that simple useless human gesture on which we all nevertheless rely so completely for what comfort this world can give.

It's been a somewhat momentous week here because I finally finished the first draft of the *Selected Essays,* 700-plus pages, which I began working on last February, a lot of hours and days, not counting all the hours and days that went into the original writing of the pieces. I've never felt so relieved to get a book off my back. It's as if I've been carrying my whole life in a grain sack over my shoulder, trudging from the loft to the manger. Now it's on the way to the publisher. It will need a good deal more work, of course, it's much too long, but I can't do that myself at this point, so I must depend on others. The whole thing seems pointless, irrelevant, futile to me now. A constant reminder of the poets who have been important to me, Jim Cunningham, Paul Goodman, Delmore Schwartz, Leonie Adams, Louise Bogan, David Ignatow, and who cares about any of them now? —we are all dead as dodoes. Don's poem about the generic vanishing poet seems particularly affecting. Well, one goes on, one does what the momentum of life requires, as Ulysses did when he plowed the beach—angry, rebellious, reluctant, determined to be insane. Meanwhile one communes with one's loved ones, mostly nonverbally, and with one's cats and dogs and hills and stars.

Otherwise the week has been largely uneventful. In the middle of it I had to go to a poetry reading by a quite well-known poet whose work I found utterly trivial and whose manner of delivery was overwrought and pretentious. I squirmed, thinking of the other real poets I know who can't get any decent notice at all. Afterward I had dinner with the poet—he's a decent enough guy—and then went to the usual party, with the result that I drank more than I should have, stumbled over a chair-leg, fell and hurt my back: nothing serious but it's sore as hell. Makes walking difficult. I won't tell you the poet's name on the off chance that he's a friend of yours and/or Don's. (These intra-literary combinations are so fucking tedious and complicated!) The further result of all this is that I'm back on the wagon, and if it means not going to any more poetry readings that's okay with me.

Had a nice letter from Adrienne about her recent month-long tour during which she covered an amazing amount of ground, gave a good number of readings, and spoke with God knows how many people, mostly strangers—probably hundreds of them. I can't imagine doing such a thing myself. What it means, of course, is not only that she has achieved a remarkable status in the world, which to my mind she altogether deserves, but that after years and decades of pain and debilitation she is really well, healthy, unimpeded by physical breakdown, perhaps the way she was years ago when she and Don were students in Cambridge. I've never known her when she wasn't limping and wincing and eating aspirins by the handful. The first time I met her, exactly thirty years ago, she was on steroids and looked plump and rosy as a result, altogether unlike herself, as I discovered not long afterward when some doctor had the sense to take her off those fearsome medications.

I wish we could all get together for an old-time literary shindig with no jealousies or competitions but only the basic affection good writers have for one another.

It's been remarkably warm these past few days, temperature in the 70s, almost like summer—except that the leaves have fallen, the flowers have withered, there's no fragrance on the air. But it's nice to sit in the sun again. Thanks to the Bo (my son) I have a winter's supply of firewood at my doorstep, which makes me feel more or less secure even though many other chores ought to be done before the snow flies. I hope to spend part of the coming week outdoors, pruning, trimming, putting things to bed. But the radio is predicting snow tonight.

Love always,

𝒫,

November 10, 1994

Dear Jane,

We're all suffering from post-election-triste here, and no doubt everywhere else too. I don't know which is more depressing, the massive stupidity and blindness of the people or the lack of leaders who can truly lead and educate. We've had nothing but mediocre flyweight presidents for such a long time. Here in New York we're lamenting the loss of Mario Cuomo, who seemed a genuinely intelligent person and who vetoed the death penalty every time it was passed in the legislature. Now we'll get the death penalty and a lot of other stupidity as well, because the guy who won is clearly nothing but a scam artist playing on the inflamed sensibilities of the electorate. Well, the arts will suffer. Here and everywhere. That's not the worst of it, but it will mean a difficult change in our own sector.

It would be easy to rant about this and its greater implications. A lot of people are. But I've never been able to get any satisfaction from listening to what I already know or telling anyone else what he or she already knows. Which is why politics, or rather the business of politics, has always bored me.

Otherwise our fine autumn continues. It's colder today and the forecaster says snow is coming tonight, but the sun is out now, it's shining on my arthritic shoulder as I write this, and that's a comfort. Everything is ragged around here, I've never lived in a place of my own that looked so uncared-for. The grape vine has grown all over the apple tree, the rosebushes are scraggly, the dead foliage from the day lilies, peonies, etc., lies where it has fallen, etc. A few days ago two former students of mine visited and they could see that the place doesn't look the way it used to; they volunteered to come and work for a while. But I told them now, if I can't keep up the place by myself, then the hell with it, I don't care. The last concord grapes on the vine, incidentally, after a few frosts, are the most delicious.

A flock of geese just flew over, heading south. Talking their mysterious language in the sky.

I spent two hours in the dentist's chair yesterday afternoon. The girls in the office make a joke of it. "Why don't you bring your blanket and just stay here?" they say. Or: "Is someone holding you hostage?" Their good humor eases the pain somewhat, but does nothing to ease the financial distress, and now, after the election, we'll be lucky if we get any health care reform at all. Certainly the hope of dental (or psychiatric) coverage in Medicare has evaporated.

I'm just wandering along, not to say maundering, as usual. And I've got a lot of work to do today. I'd better quit and make my breakfast and get going.

Love,

76

November 14, 1994

My dear,

We were glad to receive your postcard, which was waiting for us yesterday when we came back from an overnight visit in Syracuse, and to know that you're in Seattle at last and the process of treatment and recovery is beginning. By the time this reaches you—assuming it is forwarded promptly—you will be in the midst of it and probably in no condition to read it. No matter. We are thinking of you. I know the ordeal will be very difficult, as difficult as anything anyone has to sustain in this life. But I have faith in your fortitude and persistence. People like us, the pathologically depressive, are stubborn, dogged, relentless, we have had to be, and if we were better at self-promotion—though of course we're not—people would call us courageous. So I simply remind you of your will and desire, which have gotten you through terrible, terrible things so far, and they'll get you through this too.

We had a touch of winter here a couple of days ago, an arctic blast driving through. I started up the woodstove for the first time, but it brought no snow and today we're back in our prolonged, lenient autumn. It's a warm day. A little windy, the dead leaves are blowing around. What's the point in raking them? None probably, except for the sake of a seasonal ritual, which is comforting. This afternoon I'll take advantage of the warm day to do a few more outdoor chores before the real winter comes, nothing essential. In fact we are in pretty good shape for winter, I hope. We have wood, fuel, provisions, the cars have been vetted, the house is tight. Soon I'll invest some of our meager savings in a snow thrower, the powerful self-starting kind, so that we can dig ourselves out when the blizzard comes.

I have three new teeth. At age 73 that's not so bad, eh?

We hope to hear more news soon, and we send you all our love in a very warm, concentrated beam, which is embracing you, believe me, at this moment and every moment.

Yours,

G,

November 17, 1994

Dear Jane,

Today according to Don is the day when your ordeal begins—not that it didn't begin a long time ago. But this will be a particularly concentrated part of it. You won't read this, or hear Don read it, until sometime later. By then you will be recovering, your strength will be returning, your anxiety will be diminishing; no doubt you'll be trying to remember the details of what happened to you—at least that's what I did after my operation last spring—and you'll be only partly successful, much will seem vague and distant. That's a rather nice feeling, as a matter of fact. We are thinking of you with great warmth of emotional energy.

We are also getting ready to go off to Albany for this panel I'm supposed to be on at the Writers Institute with Bob Creeley, Sharon Olds, Carolyn Forché. I don't look forward to this with any pleasure except that I'll be happy to see Sharon again. I like her and haven't seen her for a couple of years. It's a warm sunny day, the drive from here to Albany takes about three hours, and if one must travel away from home in order to scrounge a living, this is the way to do it. We'll return on Saturday.

And I'll write to you again then.

Love always,

𝒦,

November 20, 1994

Dear Jane,

We got back from Albany yesterday. The conference was a fiasco, as least as regards my part of it. I had never served on a "panel" before, and no one had told me ahead of time what was expected, so I went absolutely unprepared, thinking we would engage in some kind of spontaneous discussion. Instead Bob Creeley mumbled something from a prepared text which no one could understand, Carolyn Forché spoke at great length from notes which indicated that her heart is in the right place, and Sharon Olds, bless her heart, was suffering from pneumonia and read a couple of new poems. When my turn came—last, as usual—I didn't know what to do, so I read a poem. The audience responded generously and then I said: "Now I'm an old man and if you'll excuse me I have to go to the bathroom"—and I marched down from the stage, up the aisle, and disappeared. Everybody laughed and the Institute was kind enough to pay me my fee anyway, but I felt rather abashed.

It was good to see Judy Johnson again—we've been friends for many, many years but don't have much chance to see one another even though we live only two hours apart—and to see

Russell Banks, Bill Kennedy, some of my former students, etc. It was good to be with Joe-Anne. But I do not count the two days a success.

Terribly glad to be home, as ever. The animals greeted us as if we'd been gone for months on an expedition to the North Pole, and once I got the stove fired up it seemed cozy and comfortable, just the opposite of the hotel room. Now it is Sunday morning, and I'm sitting here as usual in my old chair, wearing my old dressing gown, thinking about you and the extraordinary discomfort, to say the very least, of your present existence. It makes me feel as if I should go and get the nine-pound hammer and break my own leg with it, just so I might share somehow in your pain. I would, gladly, if it would help. But it wouldn't. Blessings on you, my dear, and on your endurance, in which I have utmost faith.

Love always,

November 26, 1994

Dear Jane,

Winter has come to the Northeast while you've been in the hospital in Seattle. It's Saturday morning here. I was awakened early by Stacey barking downstairs, wanting to go out. You can tell when the dog barks to get out because she does one bark at a time, hesitantly, reluctant to call attention to herself; not the loud, machine-gun-like woof woof woof she utters when a stranger comes. After I had let her out and waited for her to come back I was so awake that I knew going back to bed would be no use, so I made coffee and began working on my new book of poems. Now I've finished a first draft of it: 135 pages, 67 poems. All dredged up from various computer files, read once, revised slightly, and copied onto one manuscript. This is more than I thought I had, enough to make a respectable new book, but I'm awfully unsure of the quality. All the poems seem the same to me. I've lost whatever ability I once had to tell an okay poem from a good one. I'll need help with that. Anyway I've finished, and I'm having some more coffee, smoking, looking out the window. It looks exactly the same out there as it did a year ago: heavy low sky, sparse snowflakes drifting down, hardly any wind, the ground and everything on it covered with a new white blanket. Typical Upstate New York winter morning. The snowflakes are so-called "lake-effect snow," caused by cold air from Canada drifting across Lake Ontario, which is only about sixty miles away. It will go on now till April. I have kept a fire in the woodstove for the past week, and it will go on till April too, or till the wood runs out (though I think I have enough). We had a truly exceptional long warm autumn with more than usual sunshine, and everyone remarks that we have no right to complain about the winter now. But they complain anyway. And a couple of days ago when I fell on the ice in the parking lot at the market and hurt my elbow, I complained too. But in general I don't mind it.

We spent Thanksgiving day in Syracuse with Stephen and Isabel Dobyns and a number of other people, Stephen's brother from Michigan, Francine Prose and her husband Howie Michels, who cooked the turkey, also Francine's mother. Also at least six or seven children, some of whom I couldn't figure out. I drank more wine than I needed to, but we had a good

81

time and I drove home safely, if a little injudiciously, that night, and tumbled into bed at one o'clock, overfed and muddled. I slept, as they say, like a log, which is an apt simile. I have plenty of old moss-grown logs in my woods, and I can assure you they hardly ever stir, even when they're dreaming.

Now the snow is falling more thickly. We may end up with a storm before the day is through. And I never got around to buying a snow thrower, as I intended to. When I made some phone calls a couple of days ago, I was told that all the dealers are sold out. That's what comes from thinking about poetry so much instead of about the real business of life. Which reminds me that someone in Albany recently told me that when he read a poem to a group of high-school students one of them raised his hand and asked: "Is that a real poem, or did you make it up?"

Now I'm beginning to fall asleep again in spite of the coffee. It's the curse of old age. I fall asleep three or four times a day, usually right here in this chair. It's hard to accomplish anything when you're always dozing off.

Much love,

P.S.
"Is that a poem, or did you make it up?" is Bob Creeley's line, which occurs in one of his books. Creeley actually was one of the participants in that conference, which was run by Bill Kennedy at his institute attached to SUNY Albany.

November 29, 1994

Dear Jane,

We had a note from Don yesterday, much delayed by the dictating/typing/mailing process, but in a penciled addendum he said your implanting procedure began on the 18th, ten days ago, which leads me to hope you are feeling better now. Don described how you and he must converse on the phone even though you're in the same room at the hospital, which in a way seems rather nice to me—I can't say exactly why. But I remember when I was with Cindy we often used to write letters to each other while we were living together in the same house, and not because we were having a quarrel, as one might expect, but rather because we wanted to say something that required more thought than we could put into a spontaneous conversation. A little distancing within intimacy is sometimes agreeable.

I think maybe what I'm trying to get at is that when one is talking with someone face-to-face one has to look at the other person, whereas if one is talking on the phone, even in the same room, one can look somewhere else as if the other person were in St. Louis and the voice alone were making the connection. In a way that's an added intimacy.

It's Tuesday here. Joe-Anne will be going down to New Jersey for her quarterly visit with her family on Thursday. I'll be going down to New York next Monday to do a thing at the New School that night, and I'll stay with Bobbie and Galway. I was just talking with him. His new book is out but Houghton Mifflin failed to print enough copies, in fact they did an absurdly small first printing, so the book is unavailable in stores and Galway can't even get any copies for his own use. So we had a little mutual run-down on publishers, the kind that is always so neat and satisfying and supportive. Apparently Galway went back to HM after all the trouble of switching to Knopf because Bobbie thought she might be accused of nepotism or at least favoritism in dealing with his books, but I think this was a mistake.

I never have these kinds of hassles. I just do what the publisher tells me to do and never complain. That's the advantage of being a country mouse. If it is an advantage.

Well, our winter came and went, rather furiously, lots of people damaged in auto crashes on the icy roads, etc., including some people right in front of our house—we live on a steep hill—and now we're having a thaw, the snow is gone, the brook is high, a brisk warm southern wind is blowing. It blew my snow shovel from the stoop half way across the orchard. When I let Stacey out this morning, she caught a glimpse of it and began barking strenuously. She has the right idea. When changes occur in the familiar world that's what you have to do: bark like hell.

We are thinking of you, loving you, embracing you very warmly and gently.

December 5, 1994

Dear Jane,

This is a little experimental. I'm on the train heading for New York, and this is the first time I've used this computer on a moving vehicle. The train sways and jiggles a good deal, but so far I seem to be able to work the keyboard without much difficulty, not much more than I have when I'm not swaying and jiggling. This is the first time I've been on a train in several years. One difference immediately noticeable is that this train has no smoking car, which is new to me—a sign of the times. I'll be on the train a full five hours, longer if the train is late, which it usually is, and why the authorities think it's okay to deprive an addict of his (her) drug for that length of time remains mysterious to me. The nature of American fascism is to be insidious.

It's a rainy, dark day, quite warm for this season. Raindrops are spattered on the train window, everything outside looks drenched. I don't know anything more depressing than a train ride through Upstate New York anyway, all these dreary little towns—right now we're passing through Dolgeville and Little Falls—the rows of small frame houses with peeling paint and filthy yards, the gloomy streets with their flickering neon signs, empty brick factories and warehouses with broken windows. In Utica where I boarded the train the station seemed to be full of homeless people, dressed in rags, carrying plastic bags full of God knows what. In the stretches between towns we pass through scrubby woods, not a mature tree in sight, just broken, storm-damaged brush and saplings. It's just as depressing as the city, come to think of it, where I'll be in five hours. But still I'd rather live in the country.

I'm feeling anxious because I'm supposed to talk about E. E. Cummings at the New School tonight, a topic on which my knowledge is defective and my ideas are squishy at best. Can I bullshit my way through it? Probably. But I'll have to have a drink or two beforehand. I'll be staying with Bobbie and Galway, but won't get to their place until after the Cummings thing is over, probably at ten o'clock. No more than a glimpse of a visit, since I'll be returning home tomorrow. But even that will be nice. I so rarely see anyone at all these days. Galway's new book is out now, and looks substantial and handsome, but I haven't read any of it yet, except for a few poems he showed me in manuscript.

Satellite dishes listing away from the wind. Tractor tires with frozen geraniums in them. Ditches full of oily water. Barns fallen down at one end, their rusty roofing metal spread higgledy-piggledy on the ground. Stacks of old railroad ties. The name of this town is Herkimer, I think.

I won't be able to print this until I get home again.

Hope you are feeling better.

Love to you both.

December 6, 1994

Dear Jane,

I'm at Galway's place, twenty-eight stories up in the sky, the hum, rattle, honk, and buzz of city life going on contintinuously out the window, reminding me that if my ears were keen enough and I stooped down over an anthill I'd hear the same thing. What a noisy universe! Last night I listened to a lot of noise anent E.E.Cummings emitted by various pedants and poets in a hall at the New School, and wondered, even while I was contributing to it, what the hell it's all about. Here at Galway's the noise we make is gratefuller to my ear, as my father used to say: good talk over coffee and pancakes for breakfast. Galway is about to go out on various errands; I'll stay here for a couple of hours until it's time to head back to Penn Station and the train home. I'll be back in my own shabby little house tonight, and I look forward to it, though at the same time I feel a little guilty because I know the city is "where it's at" and doubtless I should be living here and sashaying around to literary events like the rest of them. Can't imagine doing that, can you?

Now what I have to worry about is whether my car, which I left in a free parking lot at the station in Utica, will be there when I get back— with its tires inflated and its windows unsmashed.

It's a brisk morning in New York, high clouds with patches of blue. I've been watching the sea gulls flying among the buildings between Bleeker Street and the Hudson River. From this height it's a little like being at sea, distances are deceiving, and sometimes distance becomes lost altogether so that one has no sense of perspective, and the gulls look like ghosts of gulls or eidolons of some kind, wheeling on a flat mysterious screen. Reality turns into a painting, a work of art. Is this an effect of life in the city, all these rectangular shapes jumbled together? I don't remember anything similar in the country. City people live without distance and perspective, or rather they perceive distance and perspective only in terms of time, which is their only environment. Somewhere outside at this moment a dog is yapping, an anxious sound twenty-eight floors below on the street, and it is as clear as it would be if the dog were next door in Munnsville. Strange.

We've been speaking, last night and this morning, of you and Don. Galway has the same snapshot of you both, pinned to his bulletin board, that Joe-Anne has at home, attached to the window-curtain by her desk. I can't say it's a small world, because it definitely isn't, but it's nice to see these threads and connections holding us together even in our mutual invisibility. I remember when I first met Don—I had met you earlier in Syracuse—at Galway's place in Sheffield. Jim Wright was there too.

Galway is very busy. Writing letters, making phone calls. At the moment he is trying to connect with someone, I don't know who, in Iowa City. I think of the number of people he must know, twenty or thirty times more than I do, he is at the center of a humming network—busy, busy, busy. Work being done. I think it gives him a sense of accomplishment quite aside from his writing, and I envy that.

Later. On board the train again, heading for Utica. We're just leaving Penn Station, the train squealing through the underground channels, dim lights strolling past, God knows where. I'm used to the old railroads that used Grand Central Terminal, a magnificent building—I'm sorry to see it abandoned. Now we are out from underground and stalled, sitting beneath some huge painted signs on the brick walls of warehouses. Extraordinary litter piled just beyond the window, metal, wood, plastic garbage. The car is overheated. In the station I had two hours to kill, so ate my lunch in a restaurant next to the waiting room, an awful "teriyaki" chicken sandwich and three glasses of wine. I'm a little loaded. I wish I were at home with my cats and my fire. Not for another five hours, if I'm lucky.

But it was good to see Galway. My spirits are definitely elevated, which is what he does for me. Not he alone; you and Don do it too, Adrienne, a few other people; people who understand—how rare we are. After the nonsense of this literary palaver last evening, Galway's words of good sense, good feeling, good perspicacity were very restorative.

Do you think it's true that the values of affection, of connection, supersede political sensitivity? I worry about this. Adrienne seems to be affirming it in some of her recent writings, but I wonder if she really means it. Last night, in fact, I was the only person present to point out that Cummings was a sexist and a racist, that some of his poems are offensive, qualities which one must come to terms with, one way or another.

Now we are stalled again, next to an embankment of alder, chokecherry, fox grapes, ironwood, a dreary mini-scape. At this rate I'll be lucky if I ever get to Utica, which is not much of a place to get to.

Love, ever,

December 12, 1994

Dear Jane,

Another Monday morning. It seems as if they come about every twenty minutes. Rather boring, except that I've never been bored in my life, as far as I can remember. And at least the seasons continue to change and continue to give me pleasure—in mundane Munnsville. We are into proper winter now, no doubt of that. The temperature outside at the moment—1:01 PM—is +10° F. It was below zero last night. The landscape is covered with snow. My woodpile is a great dune of snow, which I must dig into to get fuel for my stove, and that's a nuisance. I remember the splendid woodshed I built in Vermont, it held ten full cords of firewood, it had partly open sides so that the air circulated easily among the tiers, and it had two entrances so that the wood which was put in first could also be taken out first. I made it with old lumber and metal roofing from a barn I helped to tear down, and with poles I cut myself in the woods. It wasn't a thing of beauty but it worked; the wood was dry and had a minimum of snow on it. Those were the days. I had strength and knowledge. Now all I can do is sit and remember.

I've had a number of communications from Don lately. He says you are in horrendous pain from the radiation, which is thereby a pain for me too—I hope they are giving you sufficient anodynes; I hope there is no medical or physiological reason why they can't—but in his most recent note Don also says the tests have shown some white cells in your blood, indicating that the transplant has worked. That's wonderful news. Don described how the donated marrow was delivered, the helicopter, the exchange of anonymous messages, etc., all of which seems nicely dramatic and appropriate. Of course I have hardly any understanding of what is happening to you out there, just as I have hardly any understanding of what has happened and is happening to Martha, who has been having a lot of trouble with the chemo lately but otherwise seems to be doing well. She talks to me on the phone about her tests, with great technical flourishes anent enzymes, molecules, etc., and it all goes over my head. Totally. But the other day she did say her recent CAT scan turned up no new tumors in her liver or lungs, and that's the main thing. Anyway I hope by now you are perhaps beginning to feel a little better. I hope the radiation has not done too much damage in the wrong places.

Not much is happening here. Joe-Anne is still in New Jersey and won't be back until Thursday, I'm still going to the dentist. There's incredible Christmas nonsense everywhere, awful music, plastic Santas, blinking lights, panicky greed written on everyone's faces, children screaming, etc. It is really too much, and I escape it as well as I can by staying at home. I've decided I can't buy gifts for anyone this year or probably in any future year, so I'll just go to the bank and get some currency and hand it out, here, here, and there, trusting people to forgive me. Which reminds me that on Saturday I bought a lottery ticket because the jackpot was up to $15 million, but I haven't yet checked the numbers. Maybe I'm rich and don't know it.

I've many things to do this afternoon, so I better get going.

Much love, as always,

December 31, 1994

Dear Jane,

 It's New Year's eve. About 9:30 here. I don't know if one should try to make anything of it, but at least we survived this far, and that poor guy who was shot down over North Korea is at home again, so we know at least someone is happy. This house is very quiet and not unhappy. Joe-Anne is upstairs in her room, which I call her cave, with her papers and books and keepsakes spread all around her; I'm down here in the kitchen, as usual. It's chilly and damp, a storm is on the way. The woodstove is comforting. At midnight we shall toast the new year with orange juice and raise our glasses in your (and of course Don's) direction. The reason we won't use wine is because we drank it all last night, along with everything else in the house that was potable, having a little party here with Stephen Dobyns from Syracuse and my friends Len and Nancy Roberts from Pennsylvania. We had a fine time and we're all paying for it today, I'm sure. I am. I watched football on the tube most of the afternoon and went out only once briefly, to feed the Bo's cat and see that the trailer is in good order. Len and Nancy stayed there last night, Stephen slept in Joe-Anne's room, we slept as usual on our enormous futon in a disorderly mélange of quilts, blankets, pillows, books, stray pencils, socks, underwear, spider webs, and who knows what else, the Bo is visiting his sister in Alabama, and his dog—a sturdy chow/shepherd mix named Max—is sleeping along with Stacey at my feet, one of the cats is under the stove, the other on top of the refrigerator. The electric candles are in the windows, the Christmas tree makes a pleasant glow. A snug little household, everything considered. The Bo will return home tomorrow if he isn't delayed by the storm.

It is comforting too to know that you and Don are together again in your own place, even if the quarters are temporary, and I hope this means you are now able to take a little food and are gaining strength. I hope perhaps the pain from the radiation wounds is beginning to subside.

My New Year's resolution is to write something for myself every day, or at least every day when I don't have a hangover. And not think about whether it is germane or if the language is sufficiently elegant.

The radio in the next room is playing bells or chimes from churches all over the world. In Syracuse I used to hear the bells from the university chapel and the neighborhood religious houses all the time, and found them more annoying than appealing (no pun intended). We have none in Munnsville, only the noon siren from the firehouse. Tonight the bells sound good to me.

This is the last letter I'll be able to send you for 29¢. No doubt fifty years from now people will think this an absurdly low rate for a letter, they'll probably be paying $5. But I can remember when the rate for first-class mail was 2¢ an ounce and it stayed that way for years and years. All the 2¢ stamps were the same, little red squares with George Washington's face on them—at least that's what I remember. Of course because of the holiday this letter won't go out to you until Tuesday, and God knows when it will reach you. More and more people are using faxes. I notice from his new letterhead that Don has a fax machine now too. For my part I can't bear the thought of another expensive, breakable machine in the house, so I reckon I'll go on as I have all my life, relying on the post. I can't imagine that a fax is as pleasant to receive as a letter anyways, just as letters are nicer (and far less intrusive) than phone calls.

Well, my dear, this is my wish for a happy and very successful new year for you. May it happen. For no one else do I wish it as fervently.

With love,

January 6, 1995

Dear Jane,

Already almost a week of the new year is gone. It's hard for me to assimilate, the passage of time now in old age. I live in the midst of confusion, so that time doesn't go fast, as it used to when I was on top of my life, it nearly doesn't exist, everything is the same from one day to the next, and I can't remember in the evening what I did in the morning. I sit like a frog on a lily pad in the midst of the flow. Well, not exactly. I've suffered the usual holiday increase in mail, requests, manuscripts, etc., pouring in from all the people who sweated through the fall semester in order to attend to their own writing during the break, and I've been answering what I can dutifully, as I always do. Supporting the Munnsville post office. Very nice people down there, which is my experience with all small-town post offices, the job attracts the most intelligent and pleasantest citizens of the town. And of course they like me because I buy lots of stamps and it interests them to see where my mail comes from. A letter from Hungary is a big event in Munnsville. So they greet me with smiles and jokes when I go down there, which makes my day and is just the opposite of the dour town clerk across the street, who always looks at me as if I were delinquent in my taxes. I'm beginning to catch up with my mail at any rate, and that's a blessing.

It's been quite cold for the last three days and we've had some new snow, although nowhere near as much as the people north of here, who this time got the full treatment of "lake-effect" snowfall—three feet in Watertown and Old Forge. This region is divided into "north of the Thruway" and "south of the Thruway." Probably fifty or seventy-five years ago it was "north of the Central" and "south of the Central," meaning the railroad, and before that the dividing line was the Erie Canal, and before that the Mohawk Trail, all of them man-made features of the landscape, but created essentially by Nature, by the terrain. You can go from Buffalo to Albany in a straight line without hitting any mountains or big lakes. Here in Munnsville we're about ten miles south of the Thruway, which often makes a big difference in the weather. It depends on which way the wind is blowing across Lake Ontario. So far we've had a remarkably easy winter.

And I'm feeling better and stronger, everything considered, than I have in a long while. The new year has begun well in spite of the confusion. I'm writing a little, a new poem and further explorations of autobiography, and you know how that makes one feel better. The Bo is at home again, which pleases me. And Joe-Anne is getting along well with her new shrink in Syracuse and obviously feeling less depressed than she did six months ago. The other day she said, "Every time I go to the shrink I love you more." That can be interpreted in a number of ways, but all of them seem to be auspicious, so I said, "Well, maybe he's worth a hundred dollars a shot." And I guess he is. On the other hand it's difficult to pay his bills when they come in.

The chickadees are hollering for their breakfast. I must get dressed and give it to them.

With love,

January 11, 1995

Dear Jane,

Don't know when I wrote last. I have a feeling the interval has been longer than it should have. The amount of routine work around here has increased lately, quite noticeably; my box of unanswered mail is flowing over. I remember a poem by Wendell about taking a box of unanswered letters out and burning it, the whole damn thing consumed in one gust, so to speak. But I've never had the nerve, or whatever it takes, to do the same thing. All this is complicated by the also noticeable increase in lethargy and mental dullness that seems to be what happens when you're past 70 (although I've known 90-year-olds that were full of energy). This afternoon at about 1:00 I lay down for a bit, and the next thing I knew the dog was barking, it was three hours later, and I felt as if I were made out of warm putty. I got up and staggered down to see what Stacey was barking at, and of course there was nothing, there hardly ever is. She probably heard the door being rattled by the wind.

Yesterday afternoon Joe-Anne got into an auto accident in the town of Hamilton, about ten miles south of Munnsville, when she was taking one of her retarded clients home from a meeting. No point in going into details. No one was hurt in the slightest. Technically, legally, Joe-Anne was at fault, but there were extenuating circumstances—not that it makes much difference, an accident is an accident. The client was terribly shaken and upset, completely hysterical, and that caused a problem too, getting her home finally and calmed down. Well, these things don't bother me much, episodes in the boring part of life, and I've done my best to transmit this feeling to Joe-Anne, with some success. The problem is merely the hassle, at least for me: getting the car fixed and drivable again, struggling with the insurance people, obtaining estimates, dealing with the cops, etc. All these procedures seem to me immensely more complicated than they need to be, but I suppose that's what keeps the economy going. Economists seem to have no qualms about useless work. The whole country is featherbedding.

A letter from Don that he dictated on Christmas Eve reached me yesterday, a longer delay than usual. (Don's typist needs a course in spelling, or at least a spell-check on her—or his—computer. At one time I believe Susan Arnold was working for him, but I don't know if she still is. I've more or less lost touch with Susan and Bob.) Anyway Don says that at that time you were very sick and suffering a lot. I knew this. What has been loaded onto you by necessity is dreadful and hard to account for. I do hope you're beginning to feel better now. Continuing and recurrent pain is awfully hard to take. I've talked about this with Adrienne, whose arthritis year after year was crippling, though she is better now. She mentions pain once or twice in her poems, but has never written about it at any length. I suppose one doesn't, though I don't know why. Maybe pain is one of those experiences like orgasm or a grand mal that are impossible to describe. Right now my head is hurting a lot—again!—from my awful teeth, and I try to explore it, trace the various strands of pain along their pathways, compare them for finesse and delectability. The pain in my eye is quite different from the pain in my ear, for instance. But I can't describe either of them. We need a new lexicon. Have you been able to do any writing at all, notes, fragments? They might be quite useful in a little while. Or maybe one can't write about the most distressing things at all, whatever they are. I spent nearly four awful years in the army during the war, but I've hardly ever written anything about them, or even said anything. It's an experience worth forgetting.

Well, we are thinking of you all the time, hoping as intensely as we can for your return to good health, though that, i.e., hope, is another thing hard to describe. It has a kind of visceral quality too. I'm sure Don is taking very good care of you, even if he does reproach himself for missing one of your medications. Quite understandable. Maybe he should do as the people in hospitals do, and have a "med time" with a little cart of pills and fluids to be administered, and all the instructions written out on a chart. Then he could wear a white suit and be a proper orderly. Somehow I can't quite imagine that.

Give him our best.

And love to yourself, as ever,

January 31, 1995

Dear Jane,

In a letter received yesterday Don says you are back in the apartment again and beginning to show signs of improvement. It is good news, which we accept very gratefully. We hope and believe that your pain and difficulty will continue to abate, however gradually, so that you'll be back in Wilmot in time to see the crocuses in bloom. Already one month of the new year has passed, hard to comprehend here where life is so uneventful, but it's true, and spring is not so far off at all. We've had a few cold days lately, temperatures down to zero or below at night, but it's still an extremely mild winter with not more than two inches of snow on the ground; and today much of that may disappear because the forecasters have said we'll get up to 40° or above this afternoon.

Did you feel the earthquake? I expect you did. Fortunately not a bad one according to the reports we've heard, but enough to be frightening.

Don's letter also informed us of your mother's death, which I know is an additional difficulty for you. There's nothing I can say that you aren't already well aware of, and there's nothing you can do but accept the event as natural and ordinary in human circumstance. But that doesn't make it one bit easier.

Yesterday was one of the worst days of my life without any specific symptoms or events. I was okay for a couple of hours in the morning, but then fell asleep in my chair. When I tried to get up I was so weak and my sense of balance was so ineffective that I couldn't walk. I spent the rest of the day and night in bed, dozing but not sleeping, my whole body protesting. It's just old age, I guess. The same as I've experienced in the past, gradually increasing. I must go to Nebraska next week for six days, and the prospect frightens me. I wish Joe-Anne could go with me.

The bed, incidentally (very incidentally), is a predicament for us. A couple of years ago we had the upstairs of the house redone, new walls, new windows, the floors sanded and varnished, insulation, etc. Joe-Anne had been agitating for a new big bed for some time and the Bo had a king-sized frame with a futon on it that he couldn't use in his trailer. So we seized the occasion to bring it to the house and move it in through the biggest upstairs window while the sashes were removed. Our stairs are so narrow and twisty that we couldn't get it into the bedroom any other way. But that damned futon is like a slab of concrete, very unfriendly to old bones and arthritic joints. The question is, can we get a new mattress of some kind up the stairs and the answer is no. Or can we get rid of the frame without cutting it up with a chainsaw? Again the answer is no. So we've been putting it off. Which is foolish. Something must be done. If one spends a third of life in bed, as I guess one does, then the bed needs to be at least as comfortable as a billiard table.

Well, here I am, bitching as usual, about nothing.

I've been reading a very erotic, or at least explicitly physical, novel by Mario Vargas Llosa, whose work otherwise is not familiar to me. If he does this kind of thing all the time there's something the matter with his psyche. But I suspect this novel, which is called *Praise to the Stepmother*, is an intentional tour de force, to show how clever he is at dealing with normally unacceptable material in an acceptable way. Not a bad idea for the writer. For the reader, however, it seems unnecessary, or at least it does to this one. So the question is, shall I finish reading it or take it back to the library? Obviously I should do the latter, but my puritan genes are such that I always feel compelled to finish everything, even the detestable caviar my hostess has served me in her zeal. I'll probably read the damned thing to the last page.

Stacey is upstairs looking out the bedroom window and barking. At nothing. Sometimes I think she can hear a door opening in Oneida eight miles away. Thank God I'm not as bored as she is.

A bitchy, stupid letter. I'm sorry. I'll do better next time.

Much love,

(signature)

February 19, 1995

Dear Jane,

It's Sunday morning here, temperature about 30°, mixture of sun and clouds, the snow patchy and old. We've had thaw for the past three or four days, after a considerable period of storm earlier. I've been at home for a week and have pretty well recovered from my debauch in Nebraska, have quit blaming myself for doing the things I had to do in order to get through the agenda out there. Now if I could only recover from depression, arthritis, sore teeth, poetic despair, fuzzy vision, rage, anomie, a weak bladder, and deafness, I'd be in rather good shape.

And how are you? No word from Don lately. I hope you are genuinely beginning to feel better, even if the ravages still seem great, so that from day to day you can notice at least a little difference and take encouragement from it.

Have you ever tried acu-massage? I'm not sure if that's what it's called, but massage based on the Chinese principles used in acupuncture. It has helped Martha quite a lot, and for several years she has had a Chinese woman who speaks no English (the wife of a graduate student from China) come to see her once a week. It's not curative, of course, but the comfort Martha gets from it lasts well beyond what she would get from ordinary massage. The Chinese woman does something to her ear lobe and it makes her liver feel better. Don't ask me how. I don't even believe in it. Yet if it works with Martha, as I've seen myself, there must be something in it. Not to mention two billion Chinese.

In the past week I've written 65 letters and have almost cleared up all outstanding correspondence. Not quite. The stack still has six or eight letters in it. But tomorrow is a holiday, which means a one-day respite at the mailbox, so perhaps I'll catch up entirely. This afternoon I have to watch the Daytona 500, it's obligatory. The dullest "sport" on television, yet I'm addicted to it, like millions of others who find beauty in a carburetor and enchantment in a universal joint. And since I'll probably fall asleep in the middle of it and wake up long after the race is over, the afternoon is blown. Who cares? I'm beginning to learn how to waste time. Or rather, I've already become an expert at it. After a lifetime of obsessive labor. And my wife, the lovely and extraordinary Joe-Anne, not only condones but abets my laziness and rents blood-and-guts videos for me to watch (which don't prevent me from falling asleep) and serves me ice cream and chips and snacks of all kinds. "You've earned it," she says. There's something scandalously specious in this argument, but I'm so befuddled, under her ministrations, that I can't figure it out. How can you "earn" sin?

Ah, well, I leave it up to the theologians. And to you.

Not much else to report. The dog is bored stiff. The cats have succumbed to some kind of feline hallucinations that make them race around the house like dervishes, Joe-Anne is working her ass off at her part-time job, which has become pretty nearly full-time this winter, tomorrow we'll get her car back from the repair shop after her accident, which did more damage than was originally thought (or maybe the repair guy is scamming the insurance company), which means I can have my car back again and go for an occasional drive in the hills to look at the trees and cows or go over to Hooter's for a sip of Bass and a game of eight-ball, etc. Joe-Anne saw her car yesterday at the shop. She says it is all straightened out, including the dents that were in it before the accident, and totally sanded and repainted. It looks as it did in the showroom. So we'll have a new car with 65,000 miles on it. Not bad. As for my car, it's got so much rust it looks like a monstrous aphid going down the road, but it suits me. I ain't exactly chrome-plated myself.

Love to you both, always,

February 25, 1995

Dear Jane,

The last word I had from Don, dated about a week ago, was that he thought you'd be returning to New Hampshire yesterday. I hope you made it. If not, the date isn't so important. What counts is knowing that you are going home, the doctors and Don agree on the feasibility of it, it will happen soon if it hasn't already. In my mind I've been fantasizing visions of you. Coming to the house, seeing your dog and cat, smelling the familiar smells, looking at the big old maple with a surge of affection, seeing your books, your chair, the faithful coffee machine, etc., etc. At this moment I've just gotten up myself, and I'm having my first cup of coffee. I think about you waking on your first morning at home. It must seem nearly unbelievable. And very joyful.

That's the way I felt when I first woke in this house after I had been dead in the hospital in Utica eight years ago, even though I had had the house for only a few months and was alone in it. At least it was mine.

So greetings wherever you are, and godspeed.

Maybe on the other hand you can't smell the familiar smells. That was the principal, or at least most noticeable, brain damage I suffered when I got out of the hospital: I couldn't smell or taste anything at all. But after a few months my senses returned, and I could tell a pork chop from a captain's biscuit again.

It's been snowing here for the past 24 hours or longer, we have about a foot of new snow. Big flakes are still drifting down. Fortunately it's Saturday and Joe-Anne doesn't have to work this weekend, so we can just sit indoors and look at it.

And now I must make the coffee and feed the animals. My first cup every morning is yesterday's coffee, reheated in the microwave. Even in this poor little house we are surrounded by the apparatus of the technological age, computers, microwaves, CD players, televisions. Strange. They seem as familiar and friendly as the wood-range, the eggbeaters, the Atwater Kent of years gone by.

Much love,

P.S. I'll send this to both your addresses.

Sunday, April 9, 1995

Dear Jane,

I've neglected you lately, and everyone else, too, because I've been feeling very low— no point in going into all that— and at the same time have been pushed by the deadline for the final text of the *Selected Essays*. I've been working as hard as I can. Not hard, compared to what I could do a few years ago. I keep falling asleep. I stand up, walk around, drink coffee, smoke cigarettes, talk with Joe-Anne, then go back to the computer for another attempt. But often enough I'm asleep again in another fifteen minutes. So I don't make the progress I should, and frankly don't much care.

A friend of mine in Vermont, a poet, says that he watches

the O. J. trial every day and recommends it. A good distraction, he says. I know what he means. That kind of procedural wrangle can be fascinating for me. I remember how intently I followed the McCarthy trial in the senate back in the 1950s. But my television, which can't get cable, doesn't carry the O. J. trial, and probably that's a blessing: I'd be glued to the screen all the time otherwise.

Last week a calamity in Syracuse added to all the other bleaknesses. My friend Stephen Dobyns, who is my only close friend in this part of the world, was charged with sexual harassment at the university and suspended from his job for the rest of the semester. There's a chance he will be fired altogether. Stephen behaved badly, he threw a drink in the face of a woman who had insulted him at a party, but it was not sexual harassment at all. The woman, a graduate student, is a member of the Marxist Collective, as they call themselves, a group of deconstructivist theorists who are out to destroy the creative writing program on ideological grounds. It has become a bitter, long-standing conflict, the epitome of academic intolerance. Stephen has given them an opportunity and they are pushing it for all they're worth. I don't know what will happen. Nobody does. But it's a personal set-back for Stephen and more than that for his wife Isabel, a brilliant scientist and refugee from Chile, and their three children. If it turns out that Stephen is fired, I doubt he'll be able to get another job in teaching, and I don't know what else he'll do. It's a mess.

Joe-Anne left for south Jersey yesterday, taking Stacey with her, so I'm here alone with the two cats. It's a gray chilly morning. We had such a beautiful touch of spring last month that the snow and cold now seem awful. In Wilmot too, I'm sure. I had a call from Philip Booth yesterday, and he says the weather in Castine is just as bad as it is here. He sounded depressed too. He's been reading his father's diaries, which is NOT recommended. Thank God my father didn't keep any, as far as I know. I'll probably be spending more time up in the trailer with the Bo during the next couple of weeks, and maybe I'll go visit somebody elsewhere.

But now I must get back to the essays. Tell Don thanks for his letter. I hope by now you're feeling a little better. Don says you are able to slack off a bit on the medications, and that sounds encouraging.

Love, as ever,

R.

ACKNOWLEDGMENTS

The sequence of letters concerning the mushroom (September 10, September 12, and September 14) were first published in *Tin House* literary quarterly.

The letters of April 29, June 24, July 13, September 22, and September 26 first appeared in *Lyric Poetry Review*.